D0670070

By the grace of G-d

STORY BITES

Short Stories to Savor

Dovid Zaklikowski

HASIDIC
archives

www.HasidicArchives.com
HasidicArchives@gmail.com

ISBN 978-1-944875-15-2

Design by Carasmatic Design

To my uncle
Moshe Zaklikofsky

CONTENTS

Kindness

Deeds

Challenges

Love

Decency

Health

Livelihood

Providence

Kindness

SPLIT PORTIONS

In June of 1941, Germany invaded Russia in a massive offense. Russian citizens, already war-weary, scrambled for survival amidst the chaos. Basia Gurewicz, a young wife from Moscow, purchased numerous loaves of stale bread to keep her family afloat through the difficult months ahead.

As the Germans advanced into the Soviet Union, Basia and her son fled to safety deeper in the mountains. Although supplies dwindled, the Gurewiczs' had their backup bread to curb their hunger.

Nachum Gurewicz, Basia's husband, was drafted into the Red Army and was stationed near Moscow, which the Germans bombed incessantly for months. Serving in the vicinity of a large city made it easier for him to maintain his kosher diet and adhere to Shabbos and holiday observance. He also assisted many Jews who were in need.

Nachum was admitted one day to a military hospital due to an ulcer, and Basia was duly informed by his commanding officer. Despite the perilous journey, Basia traveled to his bedside in Moscow multiple times in order to deliver kosher food to him.

Following the war, the Gurewiczs illegally crossed the border into Poland with forged passports. They eventually made their way to Victoria, Australia, where they served as pioneers of the Jewish community. In 1964, their son, Mulik, and his wife, Chava, settled in Israel. The young couple wanted to purchase an apartment, but they needed the Jewish Agency to guarantee their loan.

Mulik made numerous trips to the Jewish Agency office to obtain the loan, but the person in charge was never there. Mulik continued to visit the office regularly, until a new clerk appeared one day. Jaded by the difficulty he'd encountered until that point, he assumed he would once again be met with excuses.

The new clerk was friendlier, and upon seeing Mulik's passport, asked him a slew of questions:

"Where were you born?" *Russia.*

"Your passport lists Poland as your place of birth." *My family escaped the Soviet Union on forged passports.*

"So this passport is forged?" *No, my previous passport was forged, but I used the same information in this passport.*

The clerk then related, "I was in the Red Army during World War II, and I was hospitalized next to a man with the same family name as you. His wife would bring him food every few days, because he adhered to kosher laws."

Mulik, aghast at the coincidence, replied, "Those were my parents."

After a series of rapid-fire questions to confirm the identity of Mulik's parents, the clerk—clearly moved—said, "Do you know what your father would do once your mother left? He would split the food with me, so that I would also have kosher food to eat."

He asked Mulik to wait for a few minutes, and returned with all the necessary signatures for the loan procurement.

PRAYING WITH SHIMON

Solikah and Chaim Pachimah watched helplessly as the small discoloration on their three-year-old son's face spread into a disfiguring growth. Eventually, Shimon lost sight in one eye, then the other, and his face became severely deformed. The family, new immigrants to Israel from Morocco, were at a loss.

When doctors were unable to help, the Pachimahs adapted to the situation as best they could. They spent extra time reading to Shimon and teaching him at home, and later enrolled him in a school for the blind. In 1980, however, his health began to deteriorate once more. He decided to travel to the United States in pursuit of treatment.

He eventually settled in the Crown Heights neighborhood in Brooklyn, New York, where he became a regular at the Lubavitch study hall on Eastern Parkway. The rabbinical students there befriended and assisted him whenever he visited. They enjoyed his company and appreciated the skills he had acquired due to his disability. He had a keen sense of hearing, and recognized voices he had heard even years ago.

Shimon also attended the gatherings of the Lubavitcher Rebbe, Rabbi Menachem Mendel Schneerson (1902–1994). Though he understood little of what was said, he felt uplifted by the Chassidic melodies sung in the intermissions between the talks. Rabbi Menachem Mendel noticed his presence and often turned to him as he was leaving the large study hall, waving his hand in encouragement. Shimon, of course, could not see, but when his friends told him about the gesture, he was deeply touched.

Not everyone was equally welcoming, however. Small children were often frightened by his deformity, while others avoided looking at him.

At the time, Rabbi Menachem Mendel would join the weekday afternoon and evening services in the small upstairs study hall of "770," as it was informally known. He would sit at one of the tables facing the crowd, and would typically place his hand on his forehead, looking down while following along in the prayer book.

When Shimon was present, however, many noticed that Rabbi Menachem Mendel would refrain from putting his hand on his forehead. They speculated that perhaps Rabbi Menachem Mendel did not want to appear as if he were trying to avoid looking at Shimon's face. While Shimon was unaware of this, the message Rabbi Menachem Mendel projected to the others in attendance was significant.

During this time, Moshe Dikstein, a visitor from Israel, arrived in 770 with his son. The young boy saw Shimon in 770, and was extremely frightened of his appearance. Moshe wrote to Rabbi Menachem Mendel about the experience, and also noted the discrepancy in Rabbi Menachem Mendel's behavior during services when Shimon was present.

Next to this observation, Rabbi Menachem Mendel wrote in the margin simply: "For the love of a Jew."

A ROBBER
GIVES CHARITY

Having lost his father at a young age, Moshe Leib Erblich (1745–1807) worked to support his family, yet he looked forward to the day when he would dedicate himself to Torah studies. His hopes were realized when his mother inherited a large sum of money that would allow him to return to school.

He traveled to a yeshiva in Mikulov (located today in Czech Republic), where he befriended the city's chief rabbi, Rabbi Shmuel Shmelke (1726–1778).

One day, the rabbi's wife removed her ring while preparing to wash her hands at water pump beside her home. A local thief, watching from nearby, stole her ring and darted off. When her husband heard the commotion, he told Moshe Leib, "Quickly, chase the thief and tell him that the ring is his, but he should know that it is worth one hundred korunas and nothing less!"

The young boy pursued the thief and delivered the message. Expecting a beating, the thief was shocked by Moshe Leib's compassionate message, and decided to return the ring.

But Moshe Leib insisted, "The rabbi gave it to you as a gift with all of his heart."

Confused, the robber said, "If the rabbi is such a person, I certainly do not want any of his property."

"If you want to do something positive, purchase jewelry for an orphaned bride," Moshe Leib replied.

The thief was so moved by the experience that he decided to change his life around by earning an honest living and providing for the needy.

THE WEEKLY NOD

In the early 1950s, Mr. David Grossman owned a butcher shop in Crown Heights, Brooklyn. On Shabbos morning, he would trek some dozen blocks to his favorite synagogue, the Agudah.

The thirty-year-old World War II veteran would leave home at precisely the same time every week, that way he would meet the Lubavitcher Rebbe, who would be on his way to the ritual bath, the Karestirer mikvah, on Eastern Parkway. At 8:50 in the morning, the two men would cross paths on a street corner.

Rabbi Menachem Mendel would nod to Mr. Grossman, wish him a "Good Shabbos," and both would continue on their way. This tradition lasted several years.

One Shabbos morning in 1952, Mr. Grossman was running late. He was disappointed that he'd likely miss his rendezvous with Rabbi Menachem Mendel, but comforted himself with the promise of future opportunities.

However, to his surprise, when he arrived at their meeting spot, Rabbi Menachem Mendel was waiting for him. As usual, they acknowledged each other warmly before parting ways.

THE LOST LOAN

When Rabbi Zelig and Chaya Slonim had a son, the couple was in such dire financial straits that they could not afford a *bris* (ritual circumcision). Rabbi Zelig traveled to his friend Rabbi Shlomo Leib Eliezrav (1862–1952) in Hebron, and asked for a loan of one gold Napoleon.

Rabbi Eliezrav gladly agreed. Relieved and grateful, Rabbi Slonim took the money and headed home. When he arrived, he put his hand in his pocket to remove the coin and, to his horror, discovered that it was gone.

The single coin was intended to support his family for a week, and cover the cost of a bris. Rabbi Slonim was at a loss. "Perhaps it fell out on the way," he considered, "or did I mistakenly leave it at the Eliezrav home?"

Though it was already dark, he carefully retraced the route to his friend's house, scouring the ground for the coin. He arrived without finding it and, with a heavy heart, knocked on the door. As the door opened, Rabbi Slonim blurted out, "Perhaps I forgot the Napoleon here? I have searched everywhere, and I simply cannot find it!"

"You forgot it here. Let me get it for you," Rabbi Eliezrav said calmly.

He disappeared and returned with the coin. Rabbi Slonim was deeply relieved that he had not lost the small fortune.

The next morning, as sunlight streamed into his home, Rabbi Slonim discovered the lost Napoleon lying on the floor where it must have fallen from his pocket. He realized that Rabbi Eliezrav had willingly given up a large sum of money rather than add to his friend's anxiety.

DO NOT FORSAKE
YOUR COMMUNITY

Rabbi Moses Rosen (1912–1994), chief rabbi of Romania, toiled for his community. Throughout the reign of the Romanian dictator Nicolae Ceausescu, he maintained his position as the chief rabbi and wielded unprecedented political power, which he used for the benefit of the Jewish community.

With great pride, he oversaw the exodus of 400,000 Romanian Jews to Israel. His policy, however, was that all Jewish clergy members and ritual slaughterers first be vetted before leaving the country. In one instance, the family of the ritual slaughterer of the small Jewish community in Dorohoi had immigrated to Israel, yet Rabbi Rosen refused to permit the man to abandon his community.

On a visit to Israel, Rabbi Rosen was greeted by this man's crying family members. "How can you separate a father from his family?" they demanded.

Rabbi Rosen was torn, unsure if he should allow the man to leave his community, and, at a meeting sometime later, he posed the question to the Lubavitcher Rebbe.

Rabbi Menachem Mendel replied, "Until you are able to replace him, it is incumbent upon the slaughterer not to abandon the small Jewish community. Let him commute from Romania to Israel to be with his family, but he should return to Romania to help preserve the Jewish observance of the Dorohoi community."

KINDNESS RECEIVABLE

B orn in Lodz, Poland, Volf Greenglass (1917–2010) had grown up in a home permeated with love of Jewish learning. Sadly, his parents, followers of the Alexander Chassidic dynasty, were so poor that Volf had to forgo an education in a Jewish school to help them earn a livelihood.

Volf longed to continue his Torah studies and constantly sought opportunities to learn. In this way, he met Rabbi Zalman Schneersohn, who organized classes and Chassidic gatherings in his home in Lodz. Volf was captivated by the Chabad approach to divine service, particularly the many hours Rabbi Schneerson would spend in prayer each day. His new mentor encouraged him to apply to the yeshiva in Otwock.

Volf doubted the yeshiva would accept him, because he was already a working man, but an acquaintance told him not to worry. He should simply apply, and he would have the opportunity to prove his abilities.

He arrived in the small resort town one evening without having arranged a place to stay. As he stood in the study hall, one of the students approached him and asked if he had a bed for the night. Hearing that he didn't, the student brought him to a room and directed him to a bed where he could rest.

Volf, exhausted from his trip, immediately fell into a deep sleep. He awoke in the middle of the night to find the same student sitting in the room and reciting the traditional *Shema* prayer said before retiring. The young man prayed with such concentration that the brief prayer lasted for hours.

In the morning, Volf learned that the student was named Yosef Wineberg. The bed was his, and he had given it up for the comfort of a stranger.

TWO ARGUMENTS

Everyone was surprised to see Rabbi Levi Yitzchok of Berditchev (1740–1809) at Herschel's funeral. After all, the great rabbi almost never attended funerals. Herschel had been rich, to be sure, but Rabbi Levi Yitzchok would not be influenced by that!

"What special merit did Herschel have that you should attend his funeral?" the townspeople asked their beloved rabbi.

The merit was an unusual one, Rabbi Levi Yitzchok said. On two occasions, Herschel had been summoned to his office due to a dispute. This in itself was nothing extraordinary. Rather, it was the nature of his conflicts that set him apart.

In the town lived a very poor man who had marriage difficulties. Unable to earn a living in Berditchev, he finally decided that he would leave town and look for employment elsewhere. He knew that his wife would not agree to this, so he resorted to deception; he told his wife that Herschel had hired him as a travelling merchant, and that she should go to the factory at the end of the month to collect his paycheck.

He knew that the ruse would not last beyond the first month, but by then he would be far away. He hoped to return with enough money to earn her forgiveness.

At the end of the month, the man's wife duly presented herself at Herschel's factory and demanded her husband's pay. When the secretary refused, telling the woman her husband was not an employee, shouting ensued. Finally, Herschel himself came out to see what the commotion was about, and the woman told him the story.

"I'm very sorry," Herschel said. "It is my fault that I forgot to tell the secretary about your husband's salary." The woman left the factory with a handsome check. She received one like it every month for the next nine months.

As he had hoped, the poor man found better luck abroad. He returned home a wealthy man. After hearing the story of Herschel's "paychecks," he immediately went to the factory and offered to repay all the money.

Herschel refused to accept it. "I gave that money as charity," he told the man. "It is no longer mine."

The man did not give up, and took Herschel to Rabbi Levi Yitzchok to negotiate repayment. This was the first conflict, the rabbi told the townspeople. He did not reveal what his ruling had been.

The second time Herschel appeared in his office was because of an argument in the marketplace. A man had lost a wallet containing borrowed money. Devastated, he began wailing that he had been robbed.

Herschel happened to be passing by. "I found money this morning," he told the man. "If you tell me the exact amount you had, I will give it back to you."

The man told him the amount, including how it had been divided up in bills. Herschel went home and returned with the money a short time later.

In fact, the man *had* been robbed. The thief was close by and watched the entire scene unfold. He was so moved by Herschel's generosity that he decided to repay him. Quietly, he approached the factory owner. The thief begged, "I stole the money, and now I regret it. Please take the money back." Herschel refused, saying, as before, that the money he had given was charity and did not belong to him anymore. Eventually, the thief took Herschel to Rabbi Levi Yitzchok to resolve their disagreement.

"Because of these two conflicts," Rabbi Levi Yitzchok concluded, "I attended Herschel's funeral."

KEEPING UP
WITH THE RECLUSE

Everett was described as a genius by those who knew him, but there were few who knew him well. The young man was reclusive, often complaining that people bored him. Rabbi Leibel Posner, then a rabbinical student, was among the lucky few with whom Everett conversed freely. Still, Posner recalled, he did most of the talking during his first meeting with Everett, which lasted several hours.

Everett had many questions about religion. "How can one explain the existence of an invisible G-d?" he asked. Posner felt he could not give his brilliant friend a satisfactory answer and decided to put the question to the Lubavitcher Rebbe.

During his next private audience, Posner told Rabbi Menachem Mendel about Everett and his dilemma. In response, Rabbi Menachem Mendel said that it had become an accepted truth that all matter is composed of atoms, which are too small to be seen. Even the atoms themselves are not solid. "On the contrary, you have more empty space than solid [mass]. This desk looks like one piece of wood, but it is not. It is actually many atoms next to one another," Rabbi Menachem Mendel explained. "The fact that atoms can't be seen does not make them any less real. A person who rejects atomic theory because he cannot see an atom is considered illogical.

"There is a subway here in New York, and an elephant in Africa," Rabbi Menachem Mendel continued. "A person can imagine the elephant in the subway. However, if you live in Poland, and you do not know what an elephant or a subway is, can you imagine an elephant in a subway? If you do not know what it is, you cannot imagine it. And because you do not know what it is, does it mean that it does not exist?"

Rabbi Posner relayed this answer to Everett, and shortly thereafter, the young man agreed to come and speak to Rabbi Menachem Mendel himself. During their three-hour discussion, Rabbi Menachem Mendel encouraged him to put on *tefillin*.

A while later, Rabbi Menachem Mendel asked Rabbi Posner whether Everett was putting on tefillin. Posner called and asked, but Everett said he had never made such a promise. He had agreed only to consider putting on tefillin, but had decided not to.

Over the next several months, Rabbi Menachem Mendel periodically checked in with Posner about the young man's situation. Posner found out that Everett was in Los Angeles and decided to reach out to him there. After several attempts, he finally got him on the phone and arranged a time to meet, but Everett never showed up.

In a private audience before Posner's wedding, Rabbi Menachem Mendel again asked about the young man, and Rabbi Posner said he did not know what had become of him. Sometime later, Rabbi

Posner met a relative of Everett's and asked how he was faring. "Have you not heard?" the man said. "He committed suicide."

THE ENVELOPE
OF CASH

The young Italian student, Yaakov, didn't know much Yiddish. Rabbi Chaim Meir Bukiet (1919–1998), dean of the Central United Lubavitch Yeshiva in Brooklyn, New York, did not speak much English. Yet they managed to communicate.

Whenever the student had a question, he would get up from his place in the large study hall and make his way to the desk where the dean spent hours each day. Having asked his question, he would listen as Rabbi Bukiet answered in the mix of Yiddish and English his family affectionately called "Yinglish."

"He had a very sharp mind," Yaakov said. "There was always a new and interesting twist that he found to explain what we were learning."

Their relationship never went beyond these brief conversations in the study hall, however. Yaakov graduated and moved on to study elsewhere.

In the spring of 1991, Yaakov became engaged to a girl from Argentina. It was a joyous time, but also a stressful one. Yaakov began to worry about how he would afford their most basic needs. Indeed, the wedding day was approaching, and he had yet to put down a deposit on their apartment or purchase basic furniture.

One day, Rabbi Bukiet arrived at the study hall for the afternoon services, and noticed that the groom was looking particularly dejected. Yaakov had kept his troubles to himself, but apparently it was not hard for the elderly rabbi to guess what perturbed him.

The dean walked over to Yaakov, as if he had come just for this purpose, handed him a bank envelope filled with cash, and said, "This is to help with the upcoming wedding." Recalling his surprise and gratitude, Yaakov says what he remembers most is the "expression of benevolence" on the rabbi's face.

At the time, and for years afterward, he assumed the money came from one of the school's funds. In fact, it had been a personal gift: Rabbi Bukiet's salary. Years of involvement with charities to support the students' basic needs had given the rabbi a keen sense for when people were in distress.

It was not the first time Rabbi Bukiet came home without his salary. When his wife asked, he would say, "I don't need to worry about money. It is *blotte* [mud]." Esther, who was meticulous about cleanliness, would happily reply, "That kind of mud you can bring home anytime." To others she would say, "My rich husband gave out checks this week."

Now a father of many children, Yaakov says that if he had known where the money was from, he would not have accepted it. Certainly, Rabbi Bukiet would be glad that he did not know.

DON'T FORGET
THE WIDOW

It was Yom Kippur morning in Liozna, the hometown of Rabbi Schneur Zalman, the first Chabad Rebbe. Rabbi Schneur Zalman was known for the fervor with which he prayed, alternating between intense, silent meditation and loud outbursts of emotion.

On this holiest day of the year, entirely devoted to prayer and fasting, his disciples were doing their best to follow his lead. But Rabbi Schneur Zalman seemed preoccupied. Then, in the middle of the cantor's repetition of prayers, the disciples were shocked to see Rabbi Schneur Zalman remove his prayer shawl and walk out of the synagogue.

Several pursued him, and watched as he entered the home of a poor isolated woman who had recently given birth. There, Rabbi Schneur Zalman took wood kindling, started a fire, and cooked porridge for the woman.

Afterward, Rabbi Schneur Zalman returned to the synagogue and resumed his prayers.

He later told his astounded disciples, "Someone who saves the life of one person is considered to have saved an entire world."

When word of this incident got out, those who opposed the Chassidic movement began to refer to Rabbi Schneur Zalman derisively as "one who desecrates Yom Kippur."

In reply, Rabbi Schneur Zalman cited the Jewish law that when someone's life is in danger on Shabbos or a holiday, the most important member of the community should desecrate the holy day to emphasize the importance of saving a life.

REMEMBERING
THE PETITION

In the 1920s, Foleh Kahan traveled from Moscow to Leningrad to celebrate the High Holidays with the sixth Lubavitcher Rebbe, Rabbi Yosef Yitzchok. Informed that someone had arrived from Moscow, the Rebbe came out to greet Foleh, obviously with something on his mind.

"How is Yitzchok Michoel Alperovitch?" Rabbi Yosef Yitzchok asked, referring to another disciple who lived in Moscow. "I did not receive a letter from him."

Like thousands of others, this Chassid would submit a petition, or *pan*, to Rabbi Yosef Yitzchok before the holiday, asking the righteous man to have him in mind during holiday prayers. In fact, Yitzchok Michoel had sent a petition that year with someone, but it had not been delivered.

Foleh assured Rabbi Yosef Yitzchok that he had spoken to Yitzchok Michoel a few days before and that he was well. It was astonishing, Foleh reflected, that among so many letters, Rabbi Yosef Yitzchok had noticed the absence of one.

DISAPPEARING PAIN

Rebbetzin Rivkah Schneersohn (1833–1914) was beloved in the town of Lubavitch. She often discreetly assisted the town's sick and needy, which earned her the title "Mother of Lubavitch."

A woman once came to Rebbetzin Rivkah's home and related that her son was sick and was craving something sweet to eat. "Please give me some dried fruits for him," she said. Rebbetzin Rivkah immediately asked her assistant to prepare an assortment of dried fruits for the sick child.

The woman thanked them and departed, but something about her story struck the assistant as suspicious. That night, the assistant stopped at the woman's home, and there, sure enough, beheld the entire family in perfect health, sitting around the table drinking tea and enjoying the dried fruits with their guests.

Disturbed, the assistant went directly to inform Rebbetzin Rivkah of what she had seen. Rebbetzin Rivkah responded, "*Nu*? Thank G-d. I was pained by the child's illness. Thank G-d he is healthy."

THE LONELY MAN

Rabbi Sholom Ber Lifshitz (1928–2011) arrived in New York for a brief visit from Israel, with plans to visit Canada over the weekend. As soon as he landed, however, the Lubavitcher Rebbe's aide called to inform him that a former classmate of Lifshitz's was feeling down and lonely, and it was requested that he remain in the vicinity of New York and make efforts to visit him.

Rabbi Lipshitz did not remember much about this former classmate—the rabbi had more important things on his mind. He was the director of an educational organization in Israel, and the trip to Canada was an important part of his yearly fundraising campaign.

However, Rabbi Menachem Mendel had other plans for him, so Lifshitz affirmed that he would forego his trip. Over the next few days, he visited his friend several times, making every effort to uplift his spirits.

On Sunday, he was invited to a private audience with Rabbi Menachem Mendel, who emphasized the imperative to reach out to an ailing Jew, and showered Rabbi Lifshitz with blessings for his efforts.

Deeds

HOLY HANDS

As a child, Yane Krichievsky (1923–2020) found it difficult to adhere to Jewish observance in the Soviet Union. He wasn't allowed to attend prayer services, and didn't receive a formal Jewish education.

As an adult, he moved to Samarkand, Uzbekistan, because it was easier to practice Judaism there. He became a successful businessman and even provided Jews who refused to work on Shabbos with jobs, which they often could not find elsewhere.

He was well connected to senior officials in the local Communist regime, but, concurrently, was subject to constant surveillance, and he was often forced to stave off danger by lining the pockets of his official friends.

When his second son was born, Yane naturally wanted him to be ritually circumcised. But it was risky. A local official had threatened him with arrest and prolonged imprisonment in Siberia should he go through with it.

In the same blasé tone as the official, Yane had replied that there were no plans for a circumcision, though he would hold a celebration for his family and friends. Among those he invited to the party was a Communist functionary, Mr. Spiegel, who was known for his love of vodka.

At the event, Yane plied Spiegel with alcohol until he was inebriated. Then the circumcision began. Holding the small child was Rabbi Shmaya Maronovsky, a refined and regal Jew with a long white beard. Tears of joy rolled down his face and he thanked G-d for the privilege of being part of such a milestone. The child was named Matisyahu, after the famed Jewish hero from the story of Chanukah, who stood up to the Greek oppression and triumphed.

As the crowd dispersed, Spiegel awoke and asked, "Who was that holy man holding the child?"

Yane told him that it was a custom for a righteous person to hold the baby and give a blessing. Everyone in attendance was gripped with fear as they realized that Spiegel might have been witness to the ceremony.

A few days after the event, Yane went to Spiegel's office in hope of bribing the official to keep quiet. However, the official had suddenly retired. Yane pressed the secretary for his address, and went to his home to find out what had transpired in those few days.

"I was greatly moved by the self-sacrifice that those at your party had for Judaism," Spiegel explained, "so I decided to give up my position and begin exploring my Jewish roots."

A TEFILLIN SCARE

Shortly after World War II began, eighteen-year-old Mottel Chaiton was drafted into the Canadian Army. During the next three years, he was stationed in Halifax, Nova Scotia, and Ottawa, Ontario.

Once, his family heard he was unwell and went to visit him. When they arrived at the army base and asked for Chaiton, the soldiers said, "Oh, you're looking for our rabbi!" and proceeded to relate how the young soldier had earned the title.

On Sundays, soldiers were required to attend church, and Mottel asked that he and the other Jewish soldiers be allowed to hold Jewish services instead. When the clergyman objected because there was no Jewish chaplain, Mottel replied, "We don't need one. I will lead the services." From then on, whenever possible, Mottel organized Torah readings and prayer services on Shabbos as well.

At one point, he was tasked with assisting the commanding officer on the base, General Peterson. One of his duties was to wake the general each morning, and so he was assigned a room near the general. Once, Peterson woke early and knocked on Mottel's door, only to find the young soldier wearing tefillin and immersed in prayer. Peterson left without saying a word.

Mottel was called to the general's office later that day. He entered with some trepidation, fearing that he was about to be disciplined. Instead, the general said, "Chaiton, don't ever let me disturb your prayers again!"

At that moment, Mottel later recalled, he understood the Talmudic verse that states (Berachot 6a), "When the nations will see you with tefillin on your head, they will fear you."

FINALLY, WATER!

In the spring of 1939, Rabbi Levi Yitzchak Schneerson (1878–1944) was arrested for promoting Jewish observance in the Soviet Union. After over a month of interrogation, solitary confinement, and torture, the rabbi was sentenced to five years of exile in Chili, a small village in Kazakhstan, two thousand miles from his home in Dnepropetrovsk, Ukraine.

It was a difficult time for the rabbi and his wife, Rebbetzin Chana, who followed him into exile. There were times when they had nothing to eat. Rebbetzin Chana recalled how her husband once said that on Shabbos their hunger was satisfied by the day itself, as the Talmud states (Shabbos 119a), "There is a spice we have, and its name is Shabbos."

Even in such circumstances, the couple made every effort to maintain the high level of observance they had held back home.

Once, Rebbetzin Chana walked a long way to procure a bucket of water. As she walked home, she thought to herself, "Finally, we will have something to drink."

Her husband, however, had another reason to celebrate. "Ah, finally," he said, "we have water to [ritually] wash our hands in the morning."

THE SNOW
DIDN'T STOP HIM

Chaim "Tashkenter" Horowitz had the custom to study each day the weekly Chassidic discourses on the Torah portion by the first Chabad Rebbe.

As a fundraiser for a day school in Brunoy, France, Chaim would frequently travel throughout Europe. Usually, he took a volume of the discourses with him, but once, he found himself in Lucerne, Switzerland, without the book. He asked around in the local Jewish community, but no one had it.

In Zurich, he was certain, he would find a copy in the home of Akiva and Malka Schmerling, manufacturers of kosher Swiss cheese.

Lucerne was ordinarily a quick hour from Zurich by rail, but due to bad weather, trains were canceled. Chaim was not about to let a snowstorm derail his study plans, so he decided to hitchhike to Zurich. Eventually he found a trucker who was willing to take him, but by the time he arrived at the Schmerling home, it was three o'clock in the morning.

Chaim did not want to knock on the door or ring the bell and risk waking the children. He knew that the Schmerlings wouldn't mind if he entered unannounced, but the doors and windows were locked. Mrs. Schmerling was awakened by the rattling noise of Chaim trying to open a window and assumed a burglar was trying to break in.

She woke her husband, who found Chaim outside the door, completely drenched. Without a word, Chaim walked to the bookshelf, found the volume he needed, and sat down to study. Only after learning for a few moments did he greet his host and explain the story behind his late visit.

HOW TO GIVE CHARITY

Every Monday and Thursday, in the town of Zeolsha, Pesach Kuper would come around the synagogue to collect money for the needy. All the congregants knew about Pesach's collection, and many would drop a coin into his charity box during the brief lull in the services.

Once, the fifth Lubavitcher Rebbe, Rabbi Sholom Dovber, was in town and prayed in the same synagogue as Pesach.

After the other congregants placed their coins in the box, Pesach emptied it and brought the box to Rabbi Sholom Dovber. Pesach planned to sell the coins the holy rabbi would donate for more than their value, thereby raising more for charity.

As Rabbi Sholom Dovber prepared to place his coins in the box, Pesach said, "Please, Rebbe, have in mind [a blessing] when you place the coins in the box, for I sell the Rebbe's coins."

"There is a simple intention," Rabbi Sholom Dovber replied. "The more others give [for the coins], the better."

THE REJECTED GUEST

The festival of Sukkos was approaching, but not a single person in the town of Berditchev had an *esrog*, the citron fruit needed on the holiday. Even in a good year, citrons were difficult to find in Eastern Europe—often a whole town would perform the mitzvah with just one esrog. However, this year, on the eve of the holiday, it appeared as though they wouldn't have even a single one for the community.

As a last resort, the famed Chassidic leader Rabbi Levi Yitzchok of Berditchev (1740–1809) sent several followers to the crossroads near the town in hope that they might waylay a traveler with an esrog who would be willing to spend the holiday with them.

There, indeed, they met a man traveling home by coach with his prized citron. He sympathized with their plight, but refused to stay. He had not been home for a long time and was looking forward to spending the festival with his family. The locals pleaded with him to remain for just a few more minutes and sent an urgent message to summon Rabbi Levi Yitzchok.

The rabbi arrived and added his entreaties to those of the townspeople. Still, the man refused. Just before his carriage began to move, Rabbi Levi Yitzchok offered the man a deal: if he would remain in town for Sukkos, when he left this world, he would share Rabbi Levi Yitzchok's own chamber in Heaven.

The man accepted the offer and agreed to stay. The people returned to their holiday preparations with renewed joy. They would be able to fulfill the cherished mitzvah after all! Amidst the commotion, the guest did not notice the rabbi pulling aside his congregants, one by one, for a brief conversation.

After prayer services that evening, the guest arrived at the home of his host family for the evening meal in the sukkah, but, shockingly, they told him he could not eat with them. Bewildered, he knocked at the house next door, but they, too, refused him entrance. He begged for an explanation. After everything he had done for them, how could they refuse him the simple hospitality of a holiday meal?

The people directed him to Rabbi Levi Yitzchok. The guest walked to his house, arriving just as the rabbi was about to begin his own meal. Frustrated and hungry, the man complained bitterly about the rude treatment he had received. Would the rabbi be willing to host him? No, Rabbi Levi Yitzchok replied, he would not be permitted in any sukkah in the town. "Unless . . ."

"*Unless what?*"

If he would forfeit his share of their deal, he would be welcome to join them, Rabbi Levi Yitzchok said.

Seeing that the rabbi had outwitted him, the man agreed.

The next day, Rabbi Levi Yitzchok invited the man back into his sukkah and explained the reason for his strange behavior. "When I first promised you a share of my spiritual reward, you were not worthy of receiving it. Only by giving it up for a chance to observe the holiday properly in *this* world could you prove yourself worthy of such a place in the World to Come."

THE TEACHER'S
PAIN AND JOY

In the summer of 1899, the ailing Rabbi
Sholom Dovber, the fifth Lubavitcher Rebbe,
was staying in a health resort town at the recommendation of his doctors. There, Rabbi Sholom
Dovber stayed in the home of a simple but pious
man who cared for his every need.

During this time, a Chassidic teacher in Beshnokovitch, whose name was also Dovber, was suddenly gripped with the desire to visit his Rebbe and
hear him speak. He traveled to Lubavitch, only to
discover that Rabbi Sholom Dovber was not there.
Nonetheless, he continued his pursuit all the way

to the resort town, where he learned that Rabbi Sholom Dovber was not speaking publicly.

Disappointed, Dovber prepared to return home. As it was too late to depart the same day, he remained in the town, and was invited to stay with a simple local Jew. Dovber initially refused to disclose the reason for his dejected spirits, but eventually revealed that he was upset he couldn't hear Rabbi Sholom Dovber speak, despite his efforts.

The host, who was close with Rabbi Sholom Dovber, immediately took his guest to the leader and described what had transpired. "When I see someone in pain, I make every effort to help," he told Rabbi Sholom Dovber.

Immediately, Rabbi Sholom Dovber delivered a discourse to the surprised and delighted audience of two.

Dovber, the teacher, thrilled by the opportunity, was simply ablaze with inspiration. His humble host, however, was somewhat envious of the intellectual delight he couldn't quite grasp. He turned to Rabbi Sholom Dovber and asked if he would experience his share of this pleasure in the World to Come.

"Perhaps," Rabbi Sholom Dovber responded, "but you should know that every time someone recites Psalms, a new [Torah] commentary is written in Heaven."

From then on, the simple man made a point of reciting Psalms with deep concentration.

THE PRAYER TRIP

There was once a businessman who prided himself on his profound prayer service. Each day, while he recited the daily service, he contemplated the Kabbalistic intentions recorded by Rabbi Isaac Luria, the Arizal. Indeed, he had become so practiced that despite this additional effort, the prayers did not take him long. He spent the rest of his time immersed in Torah study, confining his business activities to an annual trip to the marketplace in Leipzig.

The man had heard about the many hours that Rabbi Dovber, the Maggid of Mezeritch, would spend in prayer, contemplating the same intentions that he himself did. Why, he wondered, did it take the great, righteous man so long when he could do it quickly? After one of his trips to Leipzig, he decided to make a detour to Mezeritch to observe Rabbi Dovber in prayer.

Entering Rabbi Dovber's study after services, the businessman asked his question: What took Rabbi Dovber so long?

Rabbi Dovber answered in the traditional Jewish way, with another question. He asked the man how he earned his living.

"Once a year, I go to the market and purchase merchandise in which I am an expert," the man replied. "I bring it back to my city and sell it there."

"How do you know that you made a profit?" Rabbi Dovber asked.

The man explained that he keeps a detailed ledger of his accounts.

"If that is the case, why do you need to go to the market? Just fill out your ledger, and you will support yourself that way."

The man began to laugh. "Is that the way to profit, by writing down calculations? You need to actually go and do the work!"

Prayer is the same, the rabbi explained. If you do not spend the time in concentration, lifting your heart and mind into the Heavenly realms, you have not really made the required journey. Anything short of that is merely "filling out the ledger," rote recitation from which one derives no profit, "even with the best intentions in the world."

RESPECT A HOLY SPACE

The synagogue at 770 Eastern Parkway, headquarters of the Lubavitch movement, was never beautiful. The simple benches, worn tile floors, and unadorned lighting have been constants since the building was purchased in 1941.

One does not expect a boiler room to be beautiful, the Lubavitcher Rebbe's chief aide once told a visitor. Yet it serves an essential function, without which the larger structure would be uninhabitable. Similarly, he concluded, the Torah study and good deeds performed in this unpretentious building deliver light and warmth across the globe.

Still, the unpolished atmosphere in the sanctuary sometimes led people to treat it with disrespect. Rabbi Menachem Mendel, however, never forgot that a synagogue must be a dignified, clean place. He would personally pick up papers from the floor, pointing them out to others only when he could not reach them himself.

One Shabbos in the spring of 1961, Rabbi Menachem Mendel delivered a Chassidic discourse and a talk on *Ethics of Our Fathers*. "Why do the sages tell us to 'judge every person favorably'?" Rabbi Menachem Mendel asked. "Does it matter what we think privately about another person? G-d knows exactly who is right."

It matters, Rabbi Menachem Mendel said, because our thoughts affect those around us. Just as speaking ill of someone strengthens the negative traits within them, positive thoughts can "evoke the merit in the other."

At the end of the gathering, Rabbi Menachem Mendel turned to some practical business. Someone had hung up large posters in the sanctuary advertising a fundraising dinner for a Lubavitch school. "It is nice," Rabbi Menachem Mendel said, "and a good thing—for a newspaper. But in a synagogue?"

Since the event would benefit children and promote education, there was room to discuss whether the posters could be hung outside the synagogue, but within the sanctuary was not appropriate, Rabbi Menachem Mendel emphasized. Nevertheless, Rabbi Menachem Mendel instructed, they should wait until after Shabbos to remove the posters.

Challenges

THE LAST CHICKEN STANDING

Rabbi Hershel and Rochelle Fogelman had devoted a dozen years toward building the Jewish day school in Worcester, Massachusetts. After immense efforts, they were rewarded with growing enrollment and the scholastic achievements of their student body.

Not everyone in the community was pleased with the school's success, however. Several had raised objections to the Fogelmans' activities, and there was even an effort to wrest control of the school from them. In a private audience, Rabbi Fogelman told the Lubavitcher Rebbe about the situation.

Rabbi Menachem Mendel responded with a story:

Rabbi Yonasan Eibshitz, the eighteenth-century rabbinical scholar, was renowned for his brilliance and wit. He became an advisor to the king of Denmark, but their relationship was not viewed favorably by the king's other advisers. They began to discredit Rabbi Eibshitz, fabricating stories about the venerable scholar.

At the time, chicken racing was a popular sport, and the king suggested that the ministers and Rabbi Eibshitz compete in a race. Whoever's chicken prevailed would have the king's support.

The ministers fed and trained their chickens for days, and arrived at the race with large, strong birds. Rabbi Eibshitz, however, arrived with a thin, scrawny chicken, and gently placed it in the ring.

When the race began, instead of running, the larger chickens immediately began fighting with each other. They ignored the smaller bird, which feebly made its way toward the finish line and won the race.

"*Es iz gebliben nor ein dareh feigel,*" Rabbi Menachem Mendel said in Yiddish, a play on the name Fogelman, "only the one thin bird survived."

The message was clear. Those who opposed the school would ultimately exhaust themselves, and the Fogelmans need only continue their work without engaging in conflict.

BE UPLIFTED

Rabbi Yaakov Yehuda Hecht was worried. The yearly parade to bolster Jewish pride was a few days away, and he, the organizer, was not sure it would go smoothly. He worried about the weather, the floats, and the performers. Most of all, he worried about the children. Would they come? And if they came, would they enjoy it?

The day turned out to be beautiful, the parade an unqualified success. Thousands of young children showed up to see the floats depicting Jewish themes and to hear the music and speeches. The Lubavitcher Rebbe personally delivered a talk to the children and saluted the United States soldiers who participated.

As the last float disappeared from sight, Rabbi Hecht thanked the police and his staff. Rabbi Menachem Mendel, who stood beside him, added that he should thank "especially the boys and girls, children of Abraham, Isaac, Sarah, Rebecca, Rachel, and Leah."

Before Rabbi Menachem Mendel departed, Rabbi Hecht turned to him and said he hoped the parade had met Rabbi Menachem Mendel's approval. "Very much," Rabbi Menachem Mendel replied, adding, "What is with you? Why were you worried about how the parade would turn out?"

Rabbi Hecht responded, "Rebbe, you schlepped me out of my worried state!"

"Schlepped you out?" Rabbi Menachem Mendel said. "Uplifted!"

He lifted his hand above his head and repeated, "Uplifted!"

THE INVALID ESROG

With effort and great expense, the people of Berditchev had managed to obtain a single *esrog* to use on the holiday of Sukkos. The precious citrus fruit was kept in the home of the town's rabbi, Rabbi Levi Yitzchok. The townspeople were to visit the rabbi every day in order to make the blessing over the "four species."

On the first day of the festival, Rabbi Levi Yitzchok's aide began to prepare for the numerous visitors. First, Rabbi Levi Yitzchok would perform the mitzvah, followed by the other rabbis, and finally the rest of the community. Dejectedly, the aide reflected that he would likely be the last in line, despite his commitment to helping everyone else.

On the spur of the moment, he decided to make the blessing first, without anyone knowing. He seized the fruit, but it slipped through his fingers and fell to the ground. In horror, he saw that the stem had broken off, making it invalid for use.

The aide went to Rabbi Levi Yitzchok and began to weep. No one in the town would be able to perform the mitzvah, and it was his fault. He expected the rabbi to become angry. Instead, Rabbi Levi Yitzchok turned his eyes upward and exclaimed, "Master of the World! Look what kind of nation you have! They care so much for your commandments that they weep when they cannot fulfill them."

ANOTHER DAY

The elderly Shmuel Betzalel Sheftel was employed by the fifth Lubavitcher Rebbe, Rabbi Sholom Dovber, to educate his son. While Rabbi Sholom Dovber was busy with his communal duties, Shmuel Betzalel spent much of the day with the young Yosef Yitzchok.

It was his practice to tell the boy a story each evening. Once, he related a parable about a wagon driver and his teenage son. The two would wake early to transport locals to the train station. During the summer months, when the sun rose early, they would first go to morning prayers, then eat breakfast before preparing the horses.

On the fast day of the 17th of Tammuz, the father told his son that they would be skipping their meals.

At first, the hunger did not bother the young man, but by early afternoon, he became irritable and began asking his father when he would be allowed to eat. By the time the fast ended late that evening, he was simply famished, and angry with his father for forcing him to go without nourishment the entire day.

The next morning, when the father woke his son, the boy said, "I have no interest in getting out of bed. I fear that you will not let me eat again!"

"No, no, wake up!" his father said. "Today is not yesterday!"

Shmuel Betzalel then told the young boy, "These words can be applied equally to one's service of G-d ... Today is not yesterday, and each day provides us a new opportunity."

NO APOLOGY NEEDED

The name Noteh of Monastyryshche was held in reverence among people in the town of Lubavitch. Once, a Chassid arrived in town and booked a room at the local inn. When he inquired as to who else was staying there, he was told that Noteh was a guest.

The Chassid was thrilled. He had never met Noteh in person, and began asking others where he could find him. As usual, Noteh's name drew expressions of reverence and love.

One man, however, seemed unmoved. "They are making a big deal about this Noteh," he told the Chassid. "He simply lives in the small town of Monastyryshche."

The outraged Chassid began to admonish the detractor, enumerating Noteh's extraordinary qualities and urging him to show some respect. Seeing that the man remained unmoved, the Chassid slapped him across the face.

The man accepted the blow without retaliating and simply left the inn. The Chassid, meanwhile, continued searching for Noteh. He asked a man near the door if he'd seen Noteh, and was told, "He just left! Surely you saw him."

The Chassid realized that he had slapped Noteh himself. Deeply ashamed, he approached Noteh and asked for forgiveness.

With a warm smile, Noteh told him that there was no need to apologize, "What did you do to me?"

WHEN THE
ATTACKER IS RUTHLESS

During the Polish Revolution beginning in 1905, peasants and workers revolted against the government and aristocracy, demanding political freedom and better living conditions. The government resisted, and an armed struggle ensued between the army and a loose coalition of ruthless gangs.

These anarchic gangs supported their fight through robbery and extortion. They would show up at the homes of wealthy citizens and demand a large sum of money by a specific date, under threat of death. Most complied, and many Poles lived in fear of receiving a dreaded visit.

One day, a gang arrived at the home of Dovid Itkin, a real estate broker who served as custodian for several apartment buildings in Warsaw. One gang member read from a prepared document that demanded a sum of two hundred gold rubles. Dovid, who had a short temper, ripped up the paper and furiously chased the group away. A short while later, two members of the group returned, this time armed.

Dovid's wife began to wail at the top of her lungs, momentarily distracting the thugs. Dovid seized the opportunity and tackled the man with the gun. Clearly unprepared for such resistance, the two men became frightened and ran off.

Once their initial relief subsided, however, the family realized they were still in grave danger. One of Dovid's nephews suggested that he consult the fifth Lubavitcher Rebbe, Rabbi Sholom Dovber, about what he should do. Dovid traveled to the town of Lubavitch and related the entire story.

"You need to meet and make peace with them," Rabbi Sholom Dovber said, referring to the thugs.

Dovid was baffled. The gang was not an organized group with an office where he could schedule a meeting. He returned to Warsaw, but could not resume his former life. He remained at home, frightened to leave his house.

One day, his wife said that she had seen one of the gang leaders sitting in a nearby bar, and they immediately decided to go speak with him. Dovid approached the man, who had already imbibed several drinks. Dovid and his wife offered to cover his tab on condition that they would be left alone in the future. The inebriated man agreed, and the Itkins were never bothered again.

FEAR OF BELOW

After fleeing the town of Lubavitch during World War I, the fifth Lubavitcher Rebbe, Rabbi Sholom Dovber, made his way to Rostov-on-Don, a city that had only recently opened to Jewish settlement. Rabbi Sholom Dovber first moved into a second-floor apartment on Pushkinskaya Ulitsa.

On the first floor lived a Russian general who was known to be a vicious man. That Purim holiday, the crowd of disciples who came to celebrate with Rabbi Sholom Dovber were fearful lest they make too much noise and arouse the general's anger. Rabbi Sholom Dovber, however, assured everyone that there was no cause for alarm. Indeed, despite the dancing and singing well into the night, there were no complaints.

Once, one of the dishes in Rabbi Sholom Dovber's home needed to be koshered. Together with Rebbetzin Shterna Sarah, Rabbi Sholom Dovber took part in the process, pouring a large amount of boiling hot water on the dish, which overflowed and spilled all over the floor.

"There is no need to pour so much water over the floor!" the rebbetzin said hastily. "The downstairs neighbor is scary."

Rabbi Sholom Dovber responded, "Of the downstairs you are frightened. But why aren't you scared of the one Above?"

UNLIKELY DEFENDER

Shortly after his marriage, in 1954, Rabbi Abba Lerman moved to Pittsburgh, Pennsylvania, and got a job teaching in a Jewish school. He would spend the rest of his life in the classroom. A quiet, unassuming man, he saved his energy and drama for his students.

In 1962, Rabbi Lerman and his family moved to Crown Heights, from where he would commute to the Yavneh Academy in New Jersey each day. It was a turbulent time in the once-affluent Brooklyn neighborhood. Crime had become rampant, real estate prices crashed, and many Jewish residents began fleeing the area.

One evening in 1969, fourteen-year-old Avrohom Moshe Deitsch was walking down Montgomery Street when three boys armed with crowbars and sticks descended on him. They did not ask for money (he had none) but began beating him savagely. Avrohom Moshe screamed at the top of his lungs, and used the lid of a garbage can as a makeshift shield.

At first, no one responded to his calls for help. There had been several murders in the neighborhood recently, and most residents would lock their doors and windows when they heard a ruckus outside. The attackers began dragging their victim to the back of one of the houses to finish the "job" in privacy.

Rabbi Lerman, who lived nearby, had just returned home after a long day of teaching in New Jersey. Hearing screams, he opened the window and saw the young boy with blood streaming down his face, obviously losing the fight with the group of thugs. The mild-mannered teacher rushed out into the street.

Seeing new prey, the hoodlums left Avrohom Moshe alone and went after Rabbi Lerman. Several neighbors, realizing the seriousness of the situation, emerged from their homes and chased the violent teens away.

Avrohom Moshe had deep cuts on his face and head, but he was alive. Bloody and exhausted, he was brought to his home on Crown Street. His widowed mother, Mirel, was first overwhelmed, then relieved to find that he was not seriously hurt.

To show her appreciation to the teacher who had saved her son, for decades Mirel Deitsch sent him elaborate gifts every Purim. Rabbi Lerman, who would have preferred to forget the whole incident, was embarrassed by the attention. Finally, he begged her to stop, saying, "There really is no need!"

SEWING SHOES ON SHABBOS

After World War II, the Soviet Union agreed to allow Polish citizens who had fled to the USSR to return home. Religious Jews seized on this rare parting of the Iron Curtain to flee Communist oppression. In what became known as "The Great Escape," hundreds of men, women, and children posed as Polish citizens and made their way to freedom.

It was a dangerous mission that involved forging passports and paying off officials. Before one trip, the Soviet secret police caught a woman with sixty forged passports. She was jailed, but the trip was deemed too important to abandon. New passports were quickly forged, new bribes distributed, and a large group departed for the border.

In the chaos, Berel Gureveitch was left without a passport. He was arrested at the border and taken to a labor camp where he was assigned to a shoe factory.

The young man had one concern: avoiding work on Shabbos. The first week, he convinced the foreman to give him a job that did not involve sewing, one of the thirty-nine activities expressly prohibited on the holy day. The next week, however, that job was refused to him. "You have hands," the foreman said simply. "You can sew."

Berel sat, the threaded needle in his hand. He knew that if he refused to work, he would be severely punished, perhaps killed. Still, he could not bring himself to stitch the leather. Finally, he thought, "I need to try my best not to desecrate the Shabbos. G-d will do as He pleases."

He stood up and left the factory. Passing through the courtyard, he saw a group of prisoners cleaning. He said that he had been sent to join them, took a broom, and began to sweep. Soon, the foreman came looking for him, demanding to know what was going on. "If you had done some of the work, I could possibly defend you. But you did nothing. What am I supposed to tell those in charge?"

Quickly, Berel found himself standing before the factory's administrator. He, too, demanded to know why Berel had not worked. But before he could respond, the administrator asked another question, "Is it because of the Sabbath?" Berel simply shrugged, as if to say, "If you know, why even ask?"

"We have a problem," the administrator continued. "Perhaps you can help."

Leather, a rationed commodity in the USSR, was disappearing from the factory's storeroom. They had assigned guards, but they, too, had apparently stolen leather. The representative of the secret police in the factory had suggested that Berel could be relied upon not to steal.

Berel joyfully accepted the guard assignment, which allowed him to observe Shabbos fully for the remainder of his time at the camp.

POSITIVELY
COMMANDED

It was winter in 1980, and Rabbi Yaakov Winner had just arrived in Melbourne to serve as a spiritual mentor at the Rabbinical College of Australia. The role required him to lead classes and conduct Chassidic gatherings, both of which he did with the enthusiasm that characterized him.

A year after his arrival, Rabbi Winner was in a catastrophic car accident. The prognosis was not good—even if he recovered enough to function independently, the doctors said, the demanding job he had held before would be impossible.

Melbourne's Chabad community reeled. Rabbi Winner's accident was only the latest in a string of tragedies and deaths they had endured that year. Rabbi Yitzchok Dovid Groner, director of the Chabad school system in the city, began to panic. Worried that perhaps there was some kind of curse on the community, he wrote a letter to the Lubavitcher Rebbe describing his fears, and asked if there was something they should do.

Rabbi Menachem Mendel, who generally resisted the idea of connecting separate negative events, did not even address the question. Instead, he focused on Rabbi Groner's attitude, which seemed, Rabbi Menachem Mendel wrote, to evince a complete lack of faith in G-d.

Rabbi Menachem Mendel quoted the third Lubavitcher Rebbe, for whom he was named, "Think good and it will be good."

It was difficult advice to follow.

"The mood was so sour with all the recent occurrences, and to change one's mindset in the midst of tragedy was extremely difficult," Rabbi Winner recalled.

Usually, Rabbi Menachem Mendel avoided issuing direct instructions, instead offering suggestions that recipients could follow on their own initiative. For Rabbi Groner, however, Rabbi Menachem Mendel made an exception. "If you decide that it is time to fulfill the *command* [emphasis added] of our Rebbes—'Think good and it will be good'—do so in actuality," he wrote.

Rabbi Menachem Mendel was telling the community to take a leap of faith, Rabbi Winner said.

So, instead of a public reckoning, the Melbourne community embarked on a campaign of positivity. They put Rabbi Menachem Mendel's axiom to music, and sang the melody for years afterward. It did not take that long for things to improve, however. Rabbi Winner was discharged from the hospital several weeks after his accident, and made a full recovery. He continues to mentor students at the Rabbinical College to this day.

GREASING THE SOUL

The fifth Chabad Rebbe, Rabbi Sholom Dovber, suffered from medical issues and traveled often to various health resorts and clinics. On these trips, he took with him the handwritten manuscripts of his Chassidic discourses and those of his predecessors, which he would study. With such precious luggage, it was no wonder that he personally watched them being loaded into the wagons before his departure.

On one such occasion, Rabbi Sholom Dovber approached the wagon driver and asked why he waited until the wagon was full with cargo before removing the wheels and greasing the axels. "Would it not be easier to do so with less weight on them?"

The driver explained that doing it while the wagon was heavy made the grease more effective and last longer.

Rabbi Sholom Dovber then turned to his disciples and said, "This teaches us a lesson in the service of G-d: that which comes harder to us lasts longer."

Love

THE RELUCTANT DANCER

Every Friday afternoon, Rabbi Chaim Meir Bukiet, dean of the Central United Lubavitch Yeshiva, would go door-to-door on a busy commercial street in the East Flatbush neighborhood, offering to put on tefillin with the store owners and their employees. With keen understanding of human nature, he forged lifelong relationships with many.

Inspired by their father, the Bukiet children took leadership positions as Chabad emissaries and teachers around the country. Rabbi Bukiet would regularly visit his children, and for much of the last decade of his life, he spent each Chanukah and Purim in Lexington, Massachusetts, where he would dance with the crowd and teach Torah in his unique style.

The Greenbergs, a Lexington couple involved with the Chabad House, had a teenage son who was not remotely interested in Judaism. Despite their entreaties, he refused to attend services or celebrations of any kind. Once, the elder Rabbi Bukiet approached Janet Greenberg and inquired about her son's whereabouts. When she told him about his disinterest, the rabbi asked if he could speak to the boy. "It's a waste of time," Janet said.

Undaunted, Rabbi Bukiet called the teen. Mark answered, and eventually agreed to attend the Purim event, out of respect for the elderly man. The minute the young man entered the room, Rabbi Bukiet began dancing with him, stopping only when the party ended.

Mark was deeply moved by the elderly rabbi's concern for him, and he began attending Jewish community events, eventually moving on to study at the Rabbinical College of America.

THE GRASP OF A CHILD

A child once took the Lubavitcher Rebbe's hand, thinking it was his father's. Rabbi Menachem Mendel held his hand and continued walking with him. Still not realizing whose hand he held, the child wiped his face on Rabbi Menachem Mendel's coat.

When the boy's mother heard what had unfolded, she penned an apology to Rabbi Menachem Mendel, stating that she was "pained" by the incident.

Near the word *pained*, Rabbi Menachem Mendel wrote: "?!"

Then Rabbi Menachem Mendel added, "On the contrary, his act brought me great pleasure. You cannot surmise the heartiness, simplicity, innocence, and sincerity of the child—if only half these qualities could be found in an adult!"

WOOD IN THE TEFILLIN

The two brothers Rabbi Zussia of Anipoli (1708–1800) and Rabbi Elimelech of Lizensk (1717–1787) made a habit of traveling to various cities in order to encourage the Jewish inhabitants to strengthen their commitment to Torah. Their method, however, was unique. When they encountered someone who was lax in a specific area, they would stand within earshot and discuss the importance of the mitzvah. Usually, these overheard conversations had the desired effect.

Once, the brothers entered a bustling tavern and approached the stove in the center of the room. While they warmed their hands, Rabbi Zussia told Rabbi Elimelech a story. He had never checked his tefillin, he said, until recently. When the scribe had opened the boxes, he discovered that instead of parchment scrolls, they contained only wood. Rabbi Zussia began to cry, saying that he had never truly performed the mitzvah of tefillin in his life.

This was indeed a grave situation, Rabbi Elimelech told him sternly. He advised his brother to have his tefillin checked regularly from then on.

Nearby, a local man was listening intently. He went home, opened the boxes of his tefillin, and was horrified to discover that they, too, contained wood rather than parchment. In tears, he sought out the brothers, and told them what he'd found.

The brothers wrote new scrolls for the man, who was able to perform the mitzvah properly for the first time in his life. Shortly after they left town, the man passed away.

THE SHUNNED CHASSID

The city of Zembin was home to an important Lubavitch community. Many of the Chassidim who lived there had been connected to the movement since the time of Rabbi Schneur Zalman of Liadi (1745–1812), the first Chabad Rebbe.

Indeed, the locals were so concerned with maintaining their reputation for piety that when one member of the community began to drift away from Judaism, they asked him not to attend their synagogue or participate in their Torah classes.

Zembin was in the Minsk region of White Russia, close to the town of Lubavitch, where Rabbi Shmuel, the fourth Chabad Rebbe, resided. A Chassid from the town was visiting Rabbi Shmuel, when, during their private audience, Rabbi Shmuel inquired after the man who had abandoned obser-vance.

"It is not necessary to discuss him," the person responded. "We shunned him. He has been banned from our synagogue and from all our gatherings because he is a grave sinner." And he began to list the man's transgressions.

"You did not do the right thing," Rabbi Shmuel said with disappointment. "You need to befriend him. Even if your kindness will not have any effect, it is enough that he will have fewer negative thoughts throughout the day. You need to bring him closer."

RECOGNIZING
THE TREASURES

Young, idealistic, and naïve, Izzy Rosenfeld arrived in Nashville, Tennessee, in the early 1960s. He had come to assist Rabbi Zalman Posner, whose congregation, Sherith Israel, was growing. Izzy, who had little experience with Jewish life outside the hothouse environment of New York, was put in charge of youth programs, prayer services, and the Hebrew school.

He was shocked by the assimilation and apathy he encountered in Nashville. He wrote to the Lubavitcher Rebbe soon after arriving, describing his dismay at seeing community members drive to services on Shabbos, and children bringing non-kosher food to Hebrew school. When a family wanted to become more observant, he noted, the first thing they did was move to a city with more Jewish life. In such an environment, how could he convey the beauty and depth of Jewish observance to his young students?

In response, Rabbi Menachem Mendel quoted the well-known saying of the Baal Shem Tov, founder of Chassidism, that a soul may descend into this world and live for seventy or eighty years only to do a single favor for another. If this applies to a material favor, Rabbi Menachem Mendel added, how much more so should it be said of a spiritual one.

"You find yourself [in Nashville] for less than seventy or eighty days, and you already helped many Jews . . . yet you have as many complaints as the seeds of a pomegranate."

The question about how he could hope to be successful, Rabbi Menachem Mendel wrote, only a prophet could answer. Nonetheless, Rabbi Menachem Mendel had not given up hope in the Jewish nation, and he made reference to a famous teaching of the Baal Shem Tov:

> *It is written (Malachi 3:12), "For you [the Jewish nation] shall be a land of desire, says the L-rd of Hosts." Just as the greatest scholars will never discover the limits of the enormous natural resources which the Almighty has sunk into the ground, neither will anyone ever find the limits of the great treasures which lie within the Jewish nation, G-d's "land of desire."*

> *The Baal Shem Tov concluded: I want to make the Jewish nation yield the kind of produce that the Almighty's "land of desire" is capable of yielding.*

If you doubt your own abilities, you will never succeed in uncovering the "treasures" in those around you, Rabbi Menachem Mendel wrote. He concluded with instructions to continue the holy work of educating and guiding the youth.

A DIFFERENT KIND OF LOVE

When Rabbi Yitzchok Zilber (1917–2004) arrived in Israel from the Soviet Union in 1972, he was unsure what his next step should be. A mathematician by training, he wavered between working on novel theories and devoting himself to outreach in the Russian Jewish community.

He consulted several rabbis for advice, but having seen Lubavitch disciples in the USSR risk their lives to promote Jewish observance, he knew he needed to hear what Rabbi Menachem Mendel had to say.

The fifty-five-year-old rabbi saw himself, in some respects, as Rabbi Menachem Mendel's peer.

Though there were many areas in which he knew they could not be compared to one another, there was one where he suspected he might be the stronger of the two: "The Lubavitcher Rebbe surely loves Lubavitch followers more than those who are not. I am non-sectarian, and love everyone the same," he later admitted thinking to himself.

A private audience was arranged, and Rabbi Zilber spent two hours with Rabbi Menachem Mendel, relaying regards from his followers in the Soviet Union and answering Rabbi Menachem Mendel's many detailed questions about the situation of the Jews still trapped there.

When Rabbi Zilber finally had a chance to ask his question, Rabbi Menachem Mendel answered that he should put aside his scientific pursuits and dedicate himself to bringing Jews closer to Judaism, "especially Jews from the Soviet Union."

Rabbi Menachem Mendel suggested he join Shamir, an organization recently established by Chabad for this purpose. An acronym for the Hebrew words "Russian Expats, Adherents of Mitzvahs," Shamir facilitated social events and activities for Soviet refugees in Israel with a focus on Jewish observance.

Rabbi Zilber took issue with the name, however. "They may be Russian immigrants," he told Rabbi Menachem Mendel, "but we are talking about Jews who are very far from adhering to Jewish observance."

Rabbi Menachem Mendel's face became serious, and his tone changed. "Are they not circumcised? Do they not do *any* mitzvahs? How could one doubt that they adhere to *any* mitzvahs?"

From this response, Rabbi Zilber said, he understood that Rabbi Menachem Mendel's love for his fellow Jews was on a much higher level than his own.

He returned to Israel and devoted the rest of his life to Jewish outreach. Once, when someone suggested he take a break from his activities in his old age, he replied, "The Lubavitcher Rebbe told me that my soul's mission is to reach out to Russian Jews. Tell me, can I stay home while they are waiting for me?"

THE COBBLER
WHO COULD NOT LIE

It was a weekly chore young Yitzchak Shkop did not enjoy. At his father's request, every Shabbos morning he made his way to the apartment of Manis Zatnitzky in Bnei Brak, Israel. The Holocaust survivor had lost his wife and six children in the Holocaust, and though he remarried, never had more children.

Manis, who sometimes called Yitzchak "my grandson," greeted him warmly, gave him a bite to eat, and tested him on the weekly Torah portion. Still, Yitzchak would have preferred to play with his friends. When he complained, his father, Yisroel, merely replied, "If we could ease the pain of his loneliness even a little, it is worthwhile."

One day, Yisroel called his son over and said that the visits were, sadly, no longer necessary. Then he told him the following story.

In 1940, the Germans rounded up the Jews of Lodz, one of Poland's largest cities, and confined them to a ghetto. At first, the ghetto was intended as a temporary holding location for the Jews until they could be transferred to concentration camps. Soon, however, the Germans began using the Jewish population as free labor in the city's large industrial sector, producing supplies and ammunition for the war.

The shoe factory in the city was especially important. The soldiers in the German aviation, and later on the Eastern Front, were suffering from frostbite due to improperly insulated footwear. The army hoped that the insulated leather boots manufactured in Lodz would remedy the problem. Those who ran the factory were under strict instructions to accept only expert cobblers.

Yisroel, then a young man, heard that conditions in the shoe factory were good, and resolved to obtain an assignment there. He stole into the factory and went from table to table, asking if they needed help. Each time, he received a question in reply, "Are you an expert cobbler?" It was difficult for him to lie, even to save his own life. He admitted to the foremen that he was not.

There was but one work station left. Yisroel was terribly dejected, but approached the table nonetheless and inquired if he could work there. The foreman replied, "Listen, young man, there is a bucket in the corner used for coloring hides. We need someone to mix the dye to maintain its quality."

Yisroel gladly accepted his new job and immediately set to stirring the dye with one hand. After some time, the foreman asked to look at his hands. Seeing that his left hand was clean, the man yelled at him to mix with both hands. Yisroel obeyed. After a few minutes, the man came back. "Ah," he said, "now you are a cobbler. Come, join my group."

A short while later, having heard that someone had entered the factory without permission, an angry German officer stormed into the room. When the German came to the table where Yisroel was sitting, the foreman came to his defense, "This young man is here at my request. He is a professional cobbler, and I asked him to work with us." Seeing that Yisroel looked the part, as both of his hands were stained with dye, the soldier left him alone. Yisroel remained working in the factory while thousands of others were deported from the ghetto to certain death, and survived the war.

"Do you know who the foreman was?" Yisroel asked his son. "It was Manis, who just passed away. In his merit, my life was saved, and you are alive today."

Decency

THE UNWELCOME PRAISE

Once, community leader Rabbi Yaakov Yehuda Hecht was summoned to the office of the Lubavitcher Rebbe. Rabbi Menachem Mendel asked Hecht to travel to Toronto in order to mediate a dispute between two other community leaders.

Rabbi Hecht soon set off to fulfill Rabbi Menachem Mendel's bidding. The evening prior to his return to Brooklyn, he attended a relative's wedding in the city. The night wore on, and the wedding continued in full verve. Rabbi Hecht had an early flight and was anxious to get some sleep, but wanted to partake in the traditional seven blessings that are recited at the end of a wedding.

The rabbi decided to putter around the hall, and ventured to another floor where a famed Chassidic rabbi was holding personal audiences with community members. Chatting with the Chassidic leader's assistant, Rabbi Hecht commented that it was unlikely he'd sleep that night. The assistant commiserated and responded, "As we say in our circles: business before pleasure." Rabbi Hecht was bothered by the remark, as it insinuated that the Jewish tradition of reciting blessings following a wedding was simply a chore.

The wedding came to an end, and Rabbi Hecht returned to New York the following morning in time to attend prayer services with Rabbi Menachem Mendel. At the end of the services, Rabbi Menachem Mendel spotted him and asked for an update about his trip. They spoke as Rabbi Menachem Mendel walked back to his office.

Before they parted, as Rabbi Menachem Mendel was turning the key to his office, Rabbi Hecht said loudly, "How wonderful is our lot!" Rabbi Menachem Mendel turned around, and asked what he was referring to. Rabbi Hecht told Rabbi Menachem Mendel about his discussion with the Chassidic leader's assistant.

Rabbi Menachem Mendel responded, "Had I known that you would repeat *lashon harah* [negative talk], I would not have asked for an explanation."

THE ODD CHAIR

The Zirkind family home on Eastern Parkway in Brooklyn was open to anyone who needed a warm meal or some practical advice. Both the meals and the advice were dispensed at the large dining room table, which was surrounded by an assortment of mismatched chairs. It was a simple arrangement, but it served its purpose, accommodating the wide range of guests who visited each Shabbos. Amongst them was an elderly woman who came each week to chat with Rozy, the matriarch.

As a young man, Rabbi Yehuda Clapman studied daily with Rabbi Eliezer Zirkind (1931–2014), a well-known scribe. Once, Rabbi Clapman went to a furniture store, and the owner, knowing of his acquaintance with the Zirkinds, told him, "Rabbi Zirkind was just here looking for a very specific chair."

Rabbi Clapman was surprised. He knew Rabbi Zirkind as someone who paid little heed to his own physical comfort. Why, then, would he make such a purchase?

"She [the family's elderly guest] likes a certain chair," the scribe explained when Rabbi Clapman later inquired. "She told my wife she found it comfortable, so I went out and purchased one for her."

Without another word, he returned to their study routine.

DON'T BUY A TICKET

The Lubavitcher Rebbe was often asked why he remained in New York when he could have moved to Israel. To many, it seemed strange that he insisted on living in the Diaspora, especially as he professed such a strong love for the Holy Land.

Rabbi Menachem Mendel gave several answers to this question over the years, but his personal reasoning can be inferred from the response he gave when other Jewish leaders asked if they should move (paraphrased): "There is a great deal one can accomplish with the strengthening and spreading of Judaism in your community. Moreover, the need is very great, and manpower is limited. For there are relatively few who are active in this area and can be truly successful. Therefore, as a leader, you should remain where you are."

Once, someone shyly told Rabbi Menachem Mendel, "May it be G-d's will that the Rebbe should travel to the Land of Israel very soon."

Rabbi Menachem Mendel seemed surprised. "That I should travel?"

The man nodded.

"I will inquire with my secretariat if I have a plane ticket ready," Rabbi Menachem Mendel said jokingly.

As the man was about to depart, Rabbi Menachem Mendel, as if concerned that this man might indeed have taken him seriously, commented with a smile, "Please do not purchase a ticket to Israel for me."

SORE LOSER

One day, a heated argument erupted between two women who were vendors in the Bobruisk Market. Flushed and indignant, they arrived at the home of Rabbi Baruch Mordechai Ettinger, who served as the city's rabbi for five decades. The rabbi listened to them both and rendered his decision.

Unfortunately, the losing party did not take the decision well, and she began to hurl insults and profanity at the respected rabbi. Rabbi Ettinger sat patiently listening to her, but his wife was shocked. She approached her husband and demanded, "Banish this terrible person from our home!"

With a smile on his face, the rabbi replied, "Don't worry. She doesn't really mean it. It is just her anger speaking." At this, the woman became even angrier and released some more choice obscenities.

Now the rabbi's wife became angry herself and wanted to personally eject the woman from their house. But the rabbi merely turned to the raging woman and said, "Please, let me ask, do you want to have children like me?"

Without hesitating, the woman responded, "If only G-d will be so kind as to give me such children!"

"You see?" the rabbi said to his wife. "She does not really mean what she is saying."

DON'T SCARE THEM!

The Klausenberg Rebbe, Rabbi Yekusiel Yehudah Halberstam (1905–1994), lost his wife and eleven children in the Holocaust, yet he remained resilient. Even in the displaced persons camps after the war, he was active in organizing classes for children and encouraging survivors to begin their lives once more. He was known, however, to have a sharp tongue.

When he arrived in Israel, he rebuilt his community, which eventually filled an entire neighborhood. There was even a newspaper, the *Sanz Monthly*, to keep his disciples informed about community happenings, Rabbi Halberstam's talks, and family celebrations.

Late one night, Binyomin Wulliger, a diamond dealer and disciple of the Klausenberg Rebbe, received a phone call from the Lubavitcher Rebbe's office. "The Rebbe wants to know who is in charge of the *Sanz Monthly*," the secretary said. "If another person is in charge, he is asking you to pass along the message, and if you are in charge, he implores you not to publish such sharp language from Rabbi Halberstam's talks."

Binyomin said that he was not in charge, and that he didn't know what Rabbi Menachem Mendel was referring to, as he had not read the paper in its entirety.

The secretary concluded Rabbi Menachem Mendel's message to be passed on to the editor, "Sharp words dispirit people. Chassidic teachings should inspire. Print words of encouragement that will strengthen people."

YOU ARE SAFE—
THEY ARE NOT

In 1955, Rabbi David Hollander, president of the Rabbinical Council of America, decided it was time to send a delegation of rabbis to the Soviet Union to assess the situation of Soviet Jews firsthand.

He went to the Soviet embassy, and after describing his proposed trip to a clerk, he was granted permission to visit the USSR. The idea was not well received in Jewish circles, however, where many saw it as giving legitimacy to an oppressive regime. Unsure how to proceed, Rabbi Hollander sought the Lubavitcher Rebbe's advice.

At the time, the Soviet government was hostile to all religion, and practicing Judaism openly was dangerous. Those who were active in promoting observance were in even greater danger. Rabbi Menachem Mendel, who was secretly involved in numerous efforts to preserve Jewish life there, told Rabbi Hollander he should go, but gave him some advice.

"You have an American passport," Rabbi Menachem Mendel told him, "and so you are not taking much of a risk by going. But do not forget that your very presence puts others at risk. You may speak against Communist oppression in a synagogue and then return safely to the United States, while those who listen to you might be held responsible for your words. The KGB agents will ask the congregants why they let you speak, and why they associated with an American rabbi."

Rabbi Menachem Mendel continued, "You should not interpret the fact that you were given permission to visit as an indication that the government will be lenient after you leave. The people there will be careful when they come into contact with you, and you should be careful too. Don't say everything you want to say."

UNEATEN HONEY CAKE

Rabbi Yitzchok Isaac (1767–1867) was proficient in Jewish law, serving as a rabbinic authority for seventy-five years. He was known as Isaac of Vitebsk, after the city where he lived most of his long life.

Those who observed Rabbi Isaac closely noticed something unusual. On all occasions, he refused to eat honey cake. Even stranger, whenever he was questioned on the subject, Rabbi Isaac would avoid answering.

Only shortly before his passing did he explain.

At the age of twenty, just after assuming his first rabbinical position, he had attended a wedding reception. Many pastries were laid out on the table, and Rabbi Isaac took a piece of cake, made a blessing, and ate it. Someone standing nearby asked him why he had not chosen the larger and more beautiful piece of honey cake to recite the blessing on, in accordance with the law that one should recite the blessing on the best piece of food available.

"The truth is," Rabbi Isaac said, "I had forgotten about that law, but as a young rabbi, I did not want to admit my error."

Instead, he replied, "I do not eat *lekach* [honey cake]."

He may have forgotten the detail of the law, but he had never been guilty of the more serious transgression of lying. "I said I do not eat it, and I have kept my word," the rabbi emphasized.

GIVING AWAY A YEAR

In the 1970s, Chana Gurary once told Shamshon Junik, several disciples had pledged a year of their lives toward the life of her father, Rabbi Yosef Yitzchok, the sixth Lubavitcher Rebbe. This amounted to an additional thirty years, she said, adding that Rabbi Yosef Yitzchok had lived approximately thirty years after his father, Rabbi Sholom Dovber, passed away.

Upon hearing the story, Shamshon was inspired to act similarly, and wanted to "give" the seventh Lubavitcher Rebbe a year of his own life. Over the next few months he contemplated this idea, and eventually wrote to Rabbi Menachem Mendel about it.

Rabbi Menachem Mendel replied that while he appreciated the good intention, Shamshon should not involve himself in such matters. "Every year, even every day, is precious," Rabbi Menachem Mendel continued. If Shamshon used his time to the fullest, that would be "the true sacrifice."

RITUALS IN
THE BATHROOM

Rabbi Shlomo Chaim Kesselman (1894-1971) was once deep in a Chassidic gathering when a recent émigré from the Soviet Union entered the room. At the rabbi's encouragement, the man told the gathered a little about what it was like to be an observant Jew under the Communist regime.

He put on tefillin daily in secret, he said, but since he left home before daybreak, he had to bring them with him to work. "If the bosses would have seen me, I would have been fired, which would have snowballed into other issues." He would therefore go into the bathroom (a small outdoor shack), place a plank of wood over the hole, and put on tefillin.

Rabbi Kesselman was very moved by the man's self-sacrifice and the tough choices he had to make on a daily basis. But not everyone present had the same response. One of the attendees, shocked at the praise Rabbi Kesselman was heaping on the man, objected, "But it is prohibited to put on tefillin in a bathroom!"

The mentor turned to him, while the Russian Jew, who had placed his life in danger for the sole purpose of connecting to G-d as his ancestors had done, sat nearby. "Tell me," the rabbi asked, "when someone has a bathroom in his head, is he allowed to put on tefillin?"

WHO'S THE
LUCKY LADY?

Rabbi Herschel Feigelstock and Sara Esther Winter met for the first time in the fall of 1948. They liked each other despite their differences—she was an American, while he an Austrian immigrant—and since she was living in Pittsburgh and he was teaching in Montreal, they agreed to begin a correspondence.

In Montreal, the mail arrived twice a day, morning and afternoon. Sara Esther's letters, written on pink stationery, were easily recognizable, and Herschel always checked the morning mail on his way out. Sometimes, though, the mail was late. If a letter arrived from Sara Esther after Herschel left,

Rabbi Zev Greenglass, with whom Herschel was staying, would bring it to the school for him.

The pink letters were somewhat of a giveaway, so when his students once caught him reading one during a break, one of them asked, "Teacher, did you get a letter from your girlfriend?"

Six months and many letters later, the couple got engaged. When the news was out, Rabbi Greenglass approached Herschel and asked, "Who is the lucky girl?"

The young man was surprised. Was it possible that Rabbi Greenglass did not know the name of his fiancé? He had couriered her letters in his own pocket for months!

The rabbi explained, "I knew you were receiving letters from someone you were dating, but it was obvious that you didn't want me to know, so I never looked at the return address. I would never look at the name against your will."

HOLDING THE DOOR

Rabbi Dov Yehuda and Sarah Schochet emigrated from Basel, Switzerland, to Toronto with their young son, Immanuel, in the early 1950s. Toronto didn't have a suitable yeshiva at the time, so the Schochets turned to their uncle Rabbi Mordechai Aizik Hodakov, the Lubavitcher Rebbe's chief aide, for advice about where their son should study.

"If you would like to send him to school here in New York, I will look after him," Rabbi Hodakov said.

In 1952, Immanuel arrived in Brooklyn to study at the United Lubavitch Yeshiva. One week, he decided to greet Rabbi Menachem Mendel outside the central Lubavitch synagogue before Friday night services. As a newcomer, he did not realize that most attendees kept a respectful distance from Rabbi Menachem Mendel.

Rabbi Menachem Mendel did not seem to share their reticence, however. He returned Immanuel's greeting and preceded him into the synagogue. As Immanuel approached the stairs to the sanctuary, he saw that someone was holding the door open, waiting for him to enter. It was, in fact, Rabbi Menachem Mendel.

THE RICH MAN'S MEAT

Zelik Persitz, a Russian manufacturer of oil and sugar, descended from a long line of rabbinical luminaries. Though not a scholar himself, he founded many Jewish day schools and had great respect for Torah scholars, particularly the fifth Lubavitcher Rebbe, Rabbi Sholom Dovber.

Whenever Rabbi Sholom Dovber visited Moscow, Zelik made a point of calling on him at his lodgings. Once, hearing that Rabbi Sholom Dovber was at a meeting in another rabbi's home, he immediately went and waited for the meeting to finish so he would have the honor of taking Rabbi Sholom Dovber home in his wagon.

Zelik was not a Lubavitch disciple, however, and the long private audiences he had with Rabbi

Sholom Dovber differed markedly from those the Rebbe had with his disciples. At times, the conversations became heated when Zelik disagreed with Rabbi Sholom Dovber, or chose not to follow his advice. Nevertheless, the two maintained a close relationship.

Once, Rabbi Sholom Dovber was in Moscow at the same time that Zelik held a bar mitzvah celebration for his son. Hundreds of people were invited to the grand celebration, where the elite businessmen of the city mingled with important rabbis and Jewish leaders.

The meal was catered according to the most stringent kosher laws, and Rabbi Sholom Dovber, sitting in a place of honor at the head table, appeared to be partaking in the meal. But Baruch Sholom Kahan, who attended the event, noticed something unusual. "The Rebbe ate the fish, but did not bring the meat to his lips," he later told his son.

He described how Rabbi Sholom Dovber cut the meat into pieces and moved the pieces around on his plate as though he were eating. Then he would eat a piece of bread instead. It was clear to Baruch

Sholom that the Rebbe was not eating the meat because he did not know who had slaughtered it, a task he would only entrust to the most G-d-fearing Jew.

Baruch Sholom explained to his son that the Rebbe had carried out the pantomime of eating in order not to embarrass the host. Indeed, later on, the rich man took pride in how Rabbi Sholom Dovber himself had partaken in the meal.

DON'T BURN
THE BRIDGES

Max, a supporter of Chabad in Charlotte, North Carolina, was upset. There was a public dispute going on between several national Jewish organizations that he felt was unnecessary and unbecoming. While Chabad had taken a strong stance that he ultimately agreed with, he told the rabbi, "There has to be a stop to it." He wanted Chabad to compromise for the sake of Jewish unity.

"Only the [Lubavitcher] Rebbe can represent Chabad," Rabbi Groner replied, "so perhaps you should write to him."

Max wrote to Rabbi Menachem Mendel and stated his desire that the groups involved should find a way to engage in dialogue and coexist peacefully. Rabbi Menachem Mendel wrote back a very cordial letter.

As a rule, he wrote, Chabad does not respond to name-calling, and a meeting between the two parties would be pointless, "for it would place aggressor and victim in the same category, and at the [same] time, would create the impression that the leadership of your movement has done all it could and fulfilled its duty both in regard to the movement and in the eyes of the world."

Max wrote again, requesting that the groups involved meet and negotiate a compromise.

"I do not doubt your sincerity and good intentions," Rabbi Menachem Mendel responded, "but a summit between the groups would not work." Chabad was simply defending Jewish law, while the other groups had turned the disagreement into a personal feud that could not be settled through negotiation. "I would be remiss in my duties and responsibilities if I did not express my shock and disappointment at the manner in which you perceived the problem as expressed in your letter, namely as if it were a 'mutual' problem caused by two movements against each other and equally reprehensible, etc., and therefore should be 'shared personally' and mutually resolved."

Incensed at having his request denied, Max wrote a disrespectful letter to Rabbi Menachem Mendel and sent a carbon copy to Rabbi Groner. The rabbi immediately called his father, Rabbi Leib Groner, one of Rabbi Menachem Mendel's aides, and asked him to remove the letter from the mail.

The elder Rabbi Groner explained that he could not take anything out of the mail. "Whatever comes, Rabbi Menachem Mendel receives."

The Charlotte rabbi was heartbroken. He could not eat or sleep and spent the next three days reciting Psalms. When the letter finally reached New York, the elder Rabbi Groner handed it to Rabbi Menachem Mendel with trepidation. Rabbi Menachem Mendel read it and broke into a smile. Then, becoming serious, he turned to his aide, "How is your son?"

Rabbi Groner described his son's immense distress. Rabbi Menachem Mendel told him to call his son immediately and inform him that all is in order.

The younger Rabbi Groner calmed upon hearing that Rabbi Menachem Mendel was not offended. Still, he decided, he would not ask Max for the use of his pool for the Gan Israel day camp that year, as he had for many years prior.

A few days later, Rabbi Menachem Mendel asked his aide what was happening. Rabbi Groner told him about his son's decision not to ask Max for help.

"On the contrary," Rabbi Menachem Mendel said, "he needs to maintain their relationship. Do everything as it was before, and even more."

It was a difficult call for the young rabbi. He doubted whether his erstwhile supporter would even be willing to assist the camp. To his surprise, however, Max was happy to hear from him. "Everything is set up for the camp, and I cannot wait to see the kids come to our place," he said.

The update was relayed to Rabbi Menachem Mendel, and from then on, he would inquire about Max from time to time.

Today, Max's son and grandchildren are core members of their local Chabad House and attend weekly.

THE MINISTER'S RESPECT

It was 1975, and Rabbi Yaakov Yehuda Hecht was preparing to travel to London for the wedding of his son. When he informed the Lubavitcher Rebbe of his upcoming trip, he was given several tasks to fulfill while he was in the city.

Rabbi Hecht was a warm, enthusiastic, and outgoing man, especially in comparison to his more reserved British counterparts. To encourage him, Rabbi Menachem Mendel recalled a story he had been told four years prior:

In 1972, Rabbi Aron Dov Sufrin, director of education at the Lubavitch House Schools, decided to organize a student exhibition on Jewish life and history. He recruited many of the local Jewish day schools to participate, and the students put together a cutting-edge exhibit in the Lubavitch House hall.

As guest of honor for the grand opening, Rabbi Sufrin invited Lady Margaret Thatcher, then minister of education and science, and later prime minister. For two hours, the minister toured and listened to the students' detailed explanations of the exhibits.

The exhibit included a large screen with a slide-show depicting the daily life of a young Jewish girl. It started with the girl waking up, reciting the first morning prayer, washing her hands, and dressing in modest clothes.

The minister, who wore a sleeveless blouse, immediately took note. She asked her assistant to get her jacket from the car and wore it for the remainder of the visit.

Turning to Rabbi Hecht, Rabbi Menachem Mendel said, "While one can dwell on other qualities, what truly epitomizes the British is their respect for others."

SHORT-TEMPERED TEACHER

In 1946, the Gurewicz family joined a group of Chabad followers fleeing religious persecution in the Soviet Union. Using forged Polish papers, they made their way across Europe, arriving in Paris in May 1947, and resided in hotel rooms sponsored by the Jewish Joint Distribution Committee.

A small school was organized for the children in the group. The boys were taught by a teacher named Dovid, who would test the students on the material weekly. When a student did not know an answer, the teacher placed a matchstick near him. At the end of the test, unbeknownst to the parents,

Dovid would remove his belt and give each student as many lashes as the number of matchsticks he had received.

So attached was Dovid to this shocking punishment regimen that when the children stole his belt, he went on strike and refused to teach. The children utilized the time off by visiting the Eiffel Tower and other attractions in Paris. The vacation lasted two days, until the children's parents compelled them to reveal the belt's location.

Now in his eighties, Mulik Gurewicz recalls that once he had nine matches next to him when the test ended. With each blow, the teacher shouted, "A young child needs to study!" About halfway through, one of the parents walked in and, for the first time, became aware of what the teacher was using his belt for. The parent grabbed the belt, shouting, "Don't you dare give another lash!"

The parent wrote to the sixth Lubavitcher Rebbe, Rabbi Yosef Yitzchok, describing the incident. Dovid also wrote to Rabbi Yosef Yitzchok, saying, in his defense, that the students were provoking him.

Rabbi Yosef Yitzchok replied that Dovid should not teach anymore, quoting, "The short-tempered cannot teach" (*Ethics of Our Fathers* 2:5). The small school was dissolved, and the students were transferred to another school in a suburb of Paris.

LET HIM EAT IN PEACE

In 1946, the Soviets permitted Polish refugees who had fled into the USSR during the war to return home. This sparked an industry in forged Polish passports among the many who were eager to escape the oppressive Communist regime. The passports allowed people to add the names of their children, and thus people who had the prized forgeries often "adopted" new children whom they brought to freedom.

Sixteen-year-old Berel Junik was chosen to be the child of Rebbetzin Chana Schneerson on her passport, and from then on, a bond developed between the two families. Berel became a trusted helper in the homes of the rebbetzin and her son

Rabbi Menachem Mendel Schneerson, the seventh Lubavitcher Rebbe.

During the early years of Berel's service, Rabbi Menachem Mendel told him about Mendel, an aide in the home of the fifth Lubavitcher Rebbe. Whenever people probed Mendel about happenings in the Rebbe's home, he would blankly respond, "I do not know."

"If someone asks you about your work, answer that you do not know," Rabbi Menachem Mendel told him. "If you can forget everything you see, that is even better." So it was. Berel never divulged what he saw in Rabbi Menachem Mendel's home, and his commitment to confidentiality was adopted by his children, who also became involved in Rabbi Menachem Mendel's domestic life.

Rabbi Menachem Mendel and his wife, Chaya Mushka, appreciated his dedication and tried to make the work as pleasant as possible. When Berel arrived in Rabbi Menachem Mendel's home after finishing his day job in the diamond district, the rebbetzin would offer him something to eat. Berel generally accepted the offer, but if Rabbi Menachem Mendel happened to be at home, he would decline, feeling it was disrespectful to eat when Rabbi Menachem Mendel was nearby.

Once, before Rabbi Junik even had a chance to ring the bell, Rabbi Menachem Mendel realized he was at the door. Turning to the rebbetzin, he said that he would go into another room so that Berel would not see him and thus be able to eat his meal in peace. Nonetheless, Berel overheard what Rabbi Menachem Mendel said, and did not eat.

WAITING AT
THE STATION

It was 1943 in Uzbekistan, and Yaakov was eight years old. His father, Mordechai Schwei, had passed away, leaving his mother, Bunia, to raise their three sons alone. Bunia wanted the boys to have a Jewish education, but in the Soviet Union, that could land a parent in prison, or worse.

At first, she hired a private teacher, whom she paid by cleaning his home and hauling water each day from the well. But when the teacher departed for Israel (then Palestine), Bunia was at a loss. She had heard that in Samarkand there was an underground Lubavitch school. It would be too risky, however, for the entire family to travel without a permit. The boys would have to go alone.

The two older children departed, but there weren't enough funds to cover Yaakov's fare. Bunia found a man who agreed to hide the young child among the luggage, on condition that if he were discovered, the boy would say he was running away from home alone. "Don't worry," Bunia told her distraught young son. "I will soon join you in Samarkand."

Life in Samarkand was not easy for the students—accommodations were limited to a bench for a bed and one meal a day, eaten at the home of a local family. Still, they made every effort to dedicate themselves to their studies.

By the time Yaakov arrived in Samarkand, even these basics were a commodity. His older brother Isaac gave up his bench for the young boy. "That bench was your apartment," Rabbi Yaakov Schwei recalled. Isaac had arranged to eat with the same family every day, and this coveted arrangement, too, he sacrificed for his younger sibling.

Meanwhile, on the other side of the country, Bunia was making plans to join her children. One day, she was summoned to the police station. "Where is your son?" the interrogator asked her. "Why is he not in school?"

"These days, children run away from their parents," Bunia replied.

They let her go, and she sent a message to her children that she would soon make her way to Samarkand. Several weeks later, she arrived, and was surprised to see Yaakov at the station, waiting for her.

"How did you know I was coming?" she asked.

"You sent a message that you were coming," he replied, "so every day that there has been a train from our city, I have come to wait for you."

A DAILY SCHEDULE

In 1962, Jacob Hanoka was studying physics at Pennsylvania State University when he first encountered the local Hillel rabbi. The rabbi saw that Jacob was showing genuine interest in Judaism, and arranged for a group of Chabad students to host a weekend of programming on campus.

After the weekend, Jacob went to meet the Lubavitcher Rebbe. Rabbi Menachem Mendel encouraged him to take a temporary break from university and study full-time in a Jewish school, advice he eventually took.

Jacob typically had a harried schedule. He would work in the lab until midnight, and then meet friends in a bar until the wee hours of the morning. The following day, he would wake late and have lunch before heading to the lab. As such, when he transitioned to the Jewish school, he had a difficult time coping with the early start time of the classes.

During a private audience, he raised this issue with Rabbi Menachem Mendel, who responded (paraphrased), "It is important to have a daily schedule, and to eat, study, and go about your activities at a set time."

Rabbi Menachem Mendel added, "I also find this conduct helpful in my personal life."

ONE GIFT FOR TWO

Having spent his twenties fighting the Nazis as a partisan during World War II, Zushe Wilmovsky was unmarried when he moved to Israel in the early 1950s. A dedicated Chabad disciple, he quickly became involved in the movement's outreach activities in the country.

In 1952, at the age of thirty, he decided it was time to find a wife and settle down. "I purchased two suits, traveled to Jerusalem, and told a few people that I was available," he recalled years later. The strategy worked. He was introduced to Feigeh Puker, one of eleven children in a family that had roots in the Sanz Chassidic dynasty, and they wed not long after.

With little preparation, Feigeh was thrust into the life of a Chabad activist. Her husband was seldom home during the day, returning late at night, tired and hungry. His work earned him little, but Feigeh stretched and improvised to feed her family. Zushe was appreciative of her efforts, and at every meal, meager as it was, "heaped on praise about how tasty everything was," their son, Levi, recalled.

In the late 1960s, Feigeh saved up money to buy her husband a gift: a new prayer shawl. She went to the Judaica store and purchased a prayer shawl with silver embellishments, not realizing that Chabad followers eschew such adornments.

Zushe received the gift graciously, said nothing about the silver, and wore it to morning services that week.

His fellow congregants were not so discrete, however. One in particular made no effort to hide his amusement at the sight of the iconic Chabad activist wearing a non-Chabad prayer shawl. Zushe bore his jokes and comments without flinching and made no effort to defend himself.

On the way home after services, Zushe's son asked, "Father, why didn't you explain to him what happened, that you were wearing it out of respect for Mother?"

The rabbi responded, "Why does it bother you that from one deed, two people had enjoyment?"

WHERE DID
YOU FIND THE TIME?

On one of his daily bread deliveries, Meir Blizintzky unwittingly rang a celebrity's doorbell. Avigdor Hameiri, the first Poet Laureate of Israel, was delighted by the coincidence. Meir looked like someone who studied Talmud, and Avigdor was just then searching for the right Aramaic word—a word to describe a person who speaks emotionally. By way of explanation (and demonstration), Avigdor gave a spitfire tirade, which included some choice words for the sages of the Talmud.

"Listen," Meir said, "it seems that your critique is unfounded, but I have no time for discussion now. Perhaps come by my house over Shabbos."

The author accepted the invitation, and though it was an unlikely relationship, it deepened over the next three decades. At Meir's suggestion, Avigdor began sending his books to the Lubavitcher Rebbe. In 1953, he sent *The White Messiah*, a novel about a rabbi who survives the Holocaust, only to commit suicide. The book put the author's hatred for Jewish traditions, faith, and leadership on full display.

"I said that I would by this time complete your book," Rabbi Menachem Mendel wrote back to him, "and respond to you at length. However, it is difficult and distressing to read, and therefore it is taking much longer."

A few years later, in a private audience with Avigdor, Rabbi Menachem Mendel began to discuss *The White Messiah* and his other novels. It was clear that he had read them carefully. Flattered and impressed, Avigdor asked how Rabbi Menachem Mendel had found time to take an interest in his writings, which surely did not fit with the scholarly Jewish volumes that were his usual reading.

"Time," Rabbi Menachem Mendel responded, "when used properly, is unlimited."

WHEN TO KEEP QUIET

Zalman of Kurnitz was a Vilna businessman and Torah scholar who became a follower of Rabbi Schneur Zalman, founder of the Chabad movement.

Once, Zalman came to seek Rabbi Schneur Zalman's guidance about a crisis in his family: His son-in-law had an acquaintance who had recently become uncharacteristically aggressive. In an effort to help, the son-in-law had confronted him and asked why he was not acting like himself. The tactic had failed. The man tried to violently attack Zalman's son-in-law. The family was frightened that the episode might repeat itself and would end badly, he told Rabbi Schneur Zalman.

Rabbi Schneur Zalman was not sympathetic. "Do you think that this situation is totally undeserved?" he asked Zalman. "Is it incumbent on a person to express everything that he sees? I also see many things, and I keep quiet."

NOT IN PUBLIC

It was the Great Chassidic Wedding of 1806. The bride was Sheina Schneuri, granddaughter of Rabbi Schneur Zalman of Liadi; the groom, Eliezer Derbarmdiger, grandson of Rabbi Levi Yitzchok of Berditchev.

Since the two families lived far apart, the wedding was held at the halfway point, in Zlobin, Poland.

Thousands of guests descended on the city for the event. The streets around the wedding hall were teaming with well-wishers, while in the hall itself, one could hardly move. At one point, the two grandfathers wanted to discuss something privately outside, but they were unable to reach the door.

"Come," Rabbi Levi Yitzchok told Rabbi Schneur Zalman, "let us go through the wall."

Unfazed, Rabbi Schneur Zalman responded, "Not everything one is capable of should be done in public."

I DON'T WANT TO KNOW HIS NAME!

During a particularly cold and icy winter in 1980, the Lubavitcher Rebbe and his wife, Rebbetzin Chaya Mushka, began to stay in an apartment next to Lubavitch headquarters on Shabbos. Finding it convenient, they were soon spending every Shabbos and holiday at 766 Eastern Parkway.

The weekly move was carefully choreographed. Around forty minutes before candle lighting, the rebbetzin was driven to Union Street, where she took a path through the courtyard at the back of the building.

To protect her privacy, an entrance had been made there. For the most part there was no one around at that time, because the students were just returning from their weekly visits to Jews around the New York Metropolitan area.

Still, the rebbetzin, a deeply private woman, would walk quickly down the path.

As soon as Shabbos ended, while everyone was still at evening services, the rebbetzin would head to Union Street, where someone would be waiting with a car to drive her home.

One time, a young man was rushing to attend services with Rabbi Menachem Mendel, and decided to take the shortcut from Union Street at the same time that the rebbetzin was arriving. The seventeen-year-old ran straight into the rebbetzin, who grabbed onto a fence that bordered the path, averting her face. After regaining her balance, she continued on her way. By the time the student realized with whom he had collided, he could only call out his profuse apologies as she disappeared.

The next day, feeling terrible for the pain he must have caused the rebbetzin, then an octogenarian, he wrote a short note asking for forgiveness. He gave it to one of the aides who worked in the Rebbe and rebbetzin's home, asking him to give it to her.

The rebbetzin read the note with an air of disappointment. "Why did he write his name?" she asked. She did not want to have hard feelings toward him, she told the aide, even subconsciously. "I deliberately turned my face so I would not see who it was," she said.

A FACE LIKE A BEET

The crowd at the Seder table of the sixth Lubavitcher Rebbe, Rabbi Yosef Yitzchok, stared in shock. One of their fellow guests had just dipped his matzah into the beet juice on his plate, violating the Chabad custom to avoid wetting matzah lest any remaining flour within become leaven.

Seeing that the Chassidim were upset, Rabbi Yosef Yitzchok asked his aide what the problem was. The aide gave Rabbi Yosef Yitzchok a quick whispered account. "Should something be said?" he asked Rabbi Yosef Yitzchok. For the moment, at least, the guest remained oblivious.

Rabbi Yosef Yitzchok responded emphatically, "No! Better for the matzah to be red like a beet than the man's face!"

SHARING GOOD DEEDS

After illegally crossing the border from the Soviet Union after World War II, Berel Junik was living in France, dedicating himself to his studies. There he received guidance from the sixth Lubavitcher Rebbe, Rabbi Yosef Yitzchok, to become a ritual slaughterer. In 1949, with Rabbi Yosef Yitzchok's blessing, he immigrated to the United States to continue his studies. Shortly thereafter, Rabbi Yosef Yitzchok passed away.

Later that year, in a private audience, Rabbi Menachem Mendel Schneerson, son-in-law of Rabbi Yosef Yitzchok, told Berel, "My father-in-law took responsibility for you; however, [now] you need to take responsibility for yourself." The next year, when Rabbi Menachem Mendel became the seventh Lubavitcher Rebbe, Berel became a trusted aide to his family.

A quiet, reliable person, he first took responsibility for organizing the head table at which Rabbi Menachem Mendel sat during Chassidic gatherings. Later, at Rabbi Menachem Mendel's request, he began to serve meals at Rabbi Menachem Mendel's Passover table, and do other chores.

In 1952, Rabbi Menachem Mendel led a gathering after a holiday meal and asked Rabbi Junik to find someone to accompany his mother, Rebbetzin Chana, and his wife, Rebbetzin Chaya Mushka, to their homes. Rabbi Junik immediately volunteered himself for the job. "You need to do everything by yourself?" Rabbi Menachem Mendel asked with a smile.

On another occasion when he volunteered his services, Rabbi Menachem Mendel said, "Another mitzvah you are taking? Why don't you leave something for someone else?"

WHAT'S IN A NAME?

In 1966, several members of the Muskal family began to pester their brother-in-law. His name was Yaakov, as was the name of his future father-in-law, and according to the famed Rabbi Yehudah ben Shmuel of Regensburg (1150–1217), a father and son-in-law should not have the same name.

Many communities do not follow this directive, which first appeared in Rabbi Yehudah's will. Some say it was intended for his descendants, or for his students. In the Lubavitch community, however, many of the guidelines he delineated in his will are upheld. Yaakov, or Jake, as he was known, was not a Lubavitcher, but his mother and siblings had recently become followers of the Lubavitcher Rebbe.

At the time, Jake was studying at Mesivta Tiferet Yerushalayim, headed by the leading American arbiter of Jewish law, Rabbi Moshe Feinstein. Jake turned to Rabbi Feinstein for advice. Should he take on an additional name, as the family of his betrothed was suggesting? Rabbi Feinstein responded that he didn't have to. Sometime later, when Jake's future father-in-law spoke to him about the subject, Jake went to his dean again. "Tell him that if he [the senior Yaakov] wants to, he could add a name," Rabbi Feinstein said.

Shortly before the wedding, Jake's mother sent an invitation to Rabbi Menachem Mendel, and requested a blessing for the event. Seeing that both names were the same, Rabbi Menachem Mendel advised that someone should add a name.

Jake respected Rabbi Menachem Mendel. Over the years, he had several private audiences with him, of which he had warm memories. Still, he hesitated. His dean had told him that the step was unnecessary. Besides, Rabbi Menachem Mendel had not specified who should add the name. Why not his future father-in-law, since he felt so strongly about the issue?

A third time, Jake consulted Rabbi Feinstein, who seemingly had unlimited patience to hear the question over and over. Jake told him about the exchange his mother had with Rabbi Menachem Mendel.

Rabbi Feinstein finally replied, "Only out of respect for your mother, you should add a name." Jake added the name Yisroel.

CHICKEN FOR ELEVEN

When Malka married Nochum Sossonkin, he was forty and a widower with children. Despite the harsh conditions of Soviet life in the 1940s, Malka helped raise and marry off not only her husband's children, but also several of his grandchildren and relatives who were orphaned by religious persecution, famine, epidemics, and war. Rochel Kleinman, Nochum's niece, recalled how Malka welcomed her with open arms when she arrived at the Sossonkin home after her parents' deaths.

After the war, in 1946, the Sossonkins smuggled across the border into Poland. There, they learned that another relative whose husband had died in the Soviet Union had been murdered, leaving behind two young orphans. These two also joined the extended Sossonkin family.

After travelling from country to country, they arrived in Israel four years later. While they were free to practice their religion, they had little to eat. "In Paris, we had plenty of food," Rochel recalled. "In Israel, everything was rationed and limited by food cards."

The new immigrants lived in tiny quarters, with the parents sharing the little space they had with their adopted children. Despite the lack of privacy, Rochel said, a feeling of calm civility and respect for the elderly Sossonkins permeated the home. "We may have been young, but we were very mature at heart. We knew that these two righteous people were taking care of us the best that they could."

Nochum was very thoughtful and calculated in his personal life. Whenever he was served food, he would wait several minutes before beginning to eat, explaining, "When you want to eat a particular food, you need to stop for a moment and not dig in gluttonously."

At the table, he made a point of telling a story with a positive message. Often, he emphasized that all of humanity is capable of doing acts of kindness and goodness. A bus driver waiting for an elderly woman at the bus stop, a police officer greeting someone with a smile, and a stranger carrying someone's package in the street were all exhibiting divine kindness and mercy. Once, when someone was about to swat a fly, he said, "Be careful, don't end life."

Malka Sossonkin, too, made a deep impression on her young charges. "She gave to others and needed little for herself," Rochel recalled. Though Malka was caring for nine children without a washing machine, when she heard about a family with many children who needed one, she took out a loan to purchase it for them. "She taught us that if a mitzvah came our way, we should do it with joy."

On Friday nights, the family typically had one chicken to share between eleven people. Malka, the children noticed, never took a piece for herself, claiming she did not like chicken. "At one point, we refused to touch any of the chicken until she took a piece for herself," Rochel said.

It was the first time in many years that Malka Sossonkin had eaten meat.

Health

SPEEDY
IMPLEMENTATION

It was in Vienna, Austria, that the sixth Lubavitcher Rebbe, Rabbi Yosef Yitzchok, first met Dr. Joseph Wilder, a psychotherapist at the Neuropsychiatric Hospital Rosenhuegel. In 1940, when Dr. Wilder immigrated to New York, he once again treated Rabbi Yosef Yitzchok.

"When I was feeling weak and had heart pains in the evening, my primary care doctor from Vienna, Dr. Wilder, one of the great and outstanding doctors there [came to see me]," Rabbi Yosef Yitzchok wrote in 1944. "After taking medicine [he prescribed], the pain eased, and thank G-d I joined the Chassidic gathering. . . ."

In America, Dr. Wilder was a clinical professor emeritus of neurology at New York Medical College, and a founder and president of the Association for the Advancement of Psychotherapy.

Despite his busy schedule, the doctor visited Rabbi Yosef Yitzchok regularly. During one of these appointments, he mentioned new research that indicated smoking might be detrimental to health. "It was known that the Rebbe would smoke 'without matches,'" recalled Shmuel Popack, at the time a student in the Lubavitch yeshiva, "that is, lighting the first cigarette from a new pack with the last one from the previous pack, without using a match."

At the end of the examination, Dr. Wilder took out a cigarette for himself and offered one to Rabbi Yosef Yitzchok, who looked at him with surprise. The doctor may not have seriously considered the latest research, but Rabbi Yosef Yitzchok had already made a life-changing decision. "You don't know? I no longer smoke."

G-D'S PILLOW

In the early 1950s, the Goldman family lived in the Crown Heights neighborhood of Brooklyn, New York. Every day, the Lubavitcher Rebbe would pass their house on his way to and from 770 Eastern Parkway, Lubavitch headquarters.

"I couldn't help but see him when we were out on the street," Esther Goldman said. "Everybody knew who he was, what a learned person he was, and what an absolute gentleman he was."

Rabbi Menachem Mendel never failed to acknowledge her and her children, she recalled, if they happened to be outside.

On the eve of Rosh Hashanah in 1956, she had two children, Yossi and Kraindy, and was heavily pregnant with a third. While the children were playing outside, Kraindy fell down and began to cry, and Esther sprinted toward her to lift and comfort her.

Rabbi Menachem Mendel, who was passing on his way to High Holiday services, witnessed the scene unfolding. After prayers, Rabbi Menachem Mendel called her husband, Shimon, into his office and described what had happened.

"In her condition, she should not run so quickly," he said. Rabbi Menachem Mendel asked him to relay the message to his wife, adding, "When a child falls, G-d places a pillow beneath him to protect them."

ONLY HEALTH

Rabbi Sholom Dovber Schneersohn, the fifth Lubavitcher Rebbe, suffered from several ailments which made him very weak for much of his life. His poor health required him to travel to various healing spas, where he would spend months away from his cherished disciples.

Despite this, he wrote complex Chassidic discourses that are published in over forty volumes, and worked tirelessly to uphold Jewish life in Russia.

During one Chassidic gathering when Rabbi Sholom Dovber and his Chassidim were together, a Chassid named Zalman Persitz raised a cup of spirits (not his first that evening) and said, "*L'chaim,*

Rebbe! G-d should give you [health] so that you should not need to travel."

Rabbi Sholom Dovber responded, "I do not want to go. G-d is my witness. When I travel, it is like I am disconnected from life. My life is all about sharing Chassidic thought, to be given to my disciples . . ."

Nothing a person does can separate them from G-d, Rabbi Sholom Dovber continued, not even sin, because at any moment they can repent and return to G-d. One obstacle, however, cannot be overcome: "When one is sick, one cannot do anything."

A SOLDIER'S HEALTH

Rabbi Avraham Levitansky, Chabad representative to S. Monica, California, was a smoker, especially during times of high stress. During the 1970s, when he was running the local Camp Gan Israel, he was often seen with a cigarette in his hand.

One of the supporters of the camp told him several times that smoking was detrimental to his health. The camp director was courteous, but did not pay much attention to the comments. Finally, the man said, "Listen, if you don't stop, I will write to the Lubavitcher Rebbe."

"If you would like to, I cannot stop you," the rabbi replied, rather flippantly.

A short while later, around midnight, he received a phone call. It was Dr. Nissan Mindel, one of the Lubavitcher Rebbe's aides. Rabbi Menachem Mendel had asked him to relay a message: "A report arrived here that he [Levitansky] does not feel well, and that he does not take care of himself. This is very surprising, since he is an emissary, and an emissary is a soldier, and when a soldier neglects himself, it has an effect on the entire army . . ."

The camp director was surprised. "Physically, I am feeling just fine. Perhaps the Rebbe is referring to my spiritual state?"

"I was just in the Rebbe's study, and I can assure you that the Rebbe was not at all worried about the state of your spirituality," Dr. Mindel said.

Rabbi Levitansky understood the message and stopped smoking.

Livelihood

THE LONG LINE
AND THE SHORT LINE

Fleeing the Bolshevik takeover in Russia, the
Alperowitz family arrived in Jerusalem in
1924. Chaim Moshe Alperowitz was an earnest,
G-d fearing man. Those who knew him said that
not only had he never told a lie, he could not understand why anyone else would want to.

Chaim Moshe decided to become a ritual slaughterer to earn his livelihood in the new country.
There was another slaughterer in the city already,
but he was assured that there was enough business
for both of them.

He soon completed his studies and got to work.
When people heard about the new slaughterer who

had sacrificed so much to remain observant under persecution, they were eager to meet and support him, and his clientele grew rapidly.

On the eve of Yom Kippur, the line outside his home was long. Chaim Moshe, concerned that he was taking business away from the other slaughterer, sent his son to check how long the line was outside the other slaughterer's house. The boy reported back that the line was very small.

Distressed, Chaim Moshe announced that he was shuttering his business and sent everyone waiting to the home of the second slaughterer.

AN EDUCATOR
AND HIS LIVELIHOOD

It was a disaster. The new teacher at the Rishon LeZion Chabad Day School could not control his class. Rabbi Bentzion Lipskar, the Judaic principal, worried that the work he had invested in the children was being wasted.

Rishon LeZion was a first stop for many new immigrants to Israel, and the principal spent much of his time and energy helping the students acclimate to their new lives. Knowing that many children were from impoverished backgrounds and often went hungry, Rabbi Lipskar would buy fresh chicken out of his own funds several times a week for distribution to the students.

Many of the children lacked the most basic Jewish education. Rabbi Lipskar's job was made harder by parents who pulled their children out of school for menial jobs in order to ease their financial burdens.

Despite these challenges, Lipskar had succeeded in creating a functional school, only to have his work jeopardized by an incompetent teacher. After some deliberation, he decided to fire the teacher.

Rabbi Shmuel Chaim Frankel, another teacher at the school, was against the idea. "His financial situation is grave. If you fire him, he won't be able to put bread on the table," Frankel objected.

The principal dismissed this argument. "The needs cannot be mixed up," he said. "Education is education, and livelihood is livelihood. I would be the first to assist him and his family. But someone who educates young children has to be capable of the job."

A PERSONAL FAVOR

The Kahan family arrived in Israel in the mid-1930s and settled in Ramat Gan. Like most of their neighbors in the city's small Chabad community, they were extremely poor, relying on their father's milk delivery business for their meager income. "We didn't even have chairs to sit on," their son, Rabbi Yoel Kahan, recalled. "We would sit on benches around the table."

Yet the group of eight Chassidic families, mostly refugees from Communist oppression, compensated in neighborly kindness for what they lacked in material comfort. Together, they opened a school for their children, and advocated for the government to build a mikvah in their area.

One day, the father, Refoel Kahan, met Meir Blizinsky—a former classmate from their yeshiva days in Warsaw. Meir was living in Bnei Brak and employed as a house painter. Refoel urged Meir to join the fledgling community in Ramat Gan, but Meir was concerned about his livelihood.

Refoel told him not to worry, saying the community would assist.

The next day, as usual, Refoel rode from house to house on his donkey delivering milk. At each home, he asked if they would agree to purchase bread, as a personal favor, from a new delivery man who would be coming around in the future.

Many agreed, and so it was that Meir moved his family to Ramat Gan with a job already secured.

WHY IS HE POOR
WHEN SHE IS RICH?

In the early 1960s, the Tennenhaus family moved from New Brunswick to Montreal, where David Tennenhaus became director of secular studies at Beth Jacob Girls' School.

In Montreal, David met Rabbi Peretz Mochkin, who had emigrated from the Soviet Union. Rabbi Mochkin earned some money by selling homemade wine, but he was poor. Despite this, he had a zest for life and seldom complained. Still, the situation bothered David, and during a private audience with the Lubavitcher Rebbe in 1961, he raised the topic.

"Rabbi Mochkin wears a torn frock coat, and before he has a private audience with the Rebbe, he has to borrow a nice one, while Marilyn Monroe makes five million dollars a year? How could G-d allow this righteous man to live in poverty?" David asked.

Rabbi Menachem Mendel responded that Rabbi Mochkin had no interest in being rich. "I doubt if he even realizes that he has a torn frock coat. Your dilemma does not even bother him . . . While the actress you mentioned, with all of her wealth, is unhappy. She is unhappy with everything that she has."

A few months later, it became known just how unhappy Marilyn Monroe was when she committed suicide on August 5, 1962.

THE WORTHLESS EMPLOYEE

A scholar, businessman, and philanthropist, Hershel Chitrik (1927–2011) took a cool and calculated approach to business. Every venture at Citra Trading Corporation was scrutinized, the productivity of his employees was monitored, and each new hire was carefully assessed.

Yet one employee at the company seemed out of place. The man had recently lost his job, and after asking Hershel for work, had been hired on the spot. He worked in various positions, but never seemed to succeed fully in any role.

However, the man's warm personality was a positive presence at the company, so the employees tolerated and even embraced him. After some years, he fell ill with the beginning stages of an autoimmune disease. He became morose, hardly spoke, and could not work at all. Still, he continued to show up at the office every day, and Hershel continued to pay him a generous salary.

The heads of the various departments, who had long felt that the man should be replaced, finally decided to confront Hershel about the drain on the company's resources. At a weekly staff meeting, they expressed their frustration and called upon him to act.

Hershel stood up. "Does anyone know what a general ledger is?" he asked. "There are many columns. There is a column for rent, office supplies, travel, and entertainment. Then there is one for salaries, and another for charity. Just move this man's salary to the charity column. Does everybody understand?"

They moved on to the next topic, and the subject was never raised again.

BOTHERING THE PHILANTHROPIST

Benjamin Glazer, president of Advertising Arts Corporation, was a supporter of Rabbi Yosef Yitzchok, the sixth Lubavitcher Rebbe, donating tremendous sums to support Jewish activities. Over two decades, he received some sixty letters from Rabbi Yosef Yitzchok and his son-in-law Rabbi Menachem Mendel Schneerson.

"In your writing, my dear friend," Rabbi Yosef Yitzchok once wrote to him, "I feel your great spiritual pleasure and your strong will to help me in my soul-mission work. This gives me the greatest pleasure and makes it easier for me to continue [to carry] my difficult burden. . . ."

As a supporter of Chabad publishing efforts, Benjamin crossed paths with Rabbi Menachem Mendel, who then headed the Kehot Publications Society. He also had a budding relationship with Rabbi Shmaryahu Gurary, another son-in-law, who headed the network of United Lubavitch Day Schools.

When Rabbi Yosef Yitzchok passed away in 1950, it was a blow to the Lubavitch movement, leaving it fractured and in limbo. Rabbi Menachem Mendel refused to accept leadership of the movement, possibly, among other reasons, because he did not want a dispute with his older brother-in-law, who was vying for the position.

When Rabbi Menachem Mendel finally did accept leadership in 1951, Mr. Glazer was there to congratulate the new Lubavitcher Rebbe. "It was with a great deal of joy that I received the official memorandum," Glazer wrote, "of your elevation, succeeding your beloved father-in-law, Rabbi Joseph I. Schneersohn, of saintly memory. I feel very inadequate in trying to put into words what is in my heart. However, having the privilege of knowing you for a number of years, I know that Jewry will be the beneficiary of your great wisdom, piety, sincerity and deep compassion for all our fellow Jews."

Rabbi Menachem Mendel made every effort to conduct activities in a peaceful manner, and while he sent blessings to Glazer for holidays and other occasions, he did not ask for monetary help, as Glazer was a firm supporter of the day schools directed by his brother-in-law, Rabbi Gurary, and Rabbi Menachem Mendel did not want to detract from that arrangement.

However, when it came to assisting another, the new rebbe didn't hesitate. Thus, Rabbi Menachem Mendel wrote a letter on behalf of Joe Gross, a cartoonist, encouraging Glazer to meet with him.

"As the president of an advertising agency," Rabbi Menachem Mendel wrote, "I would appreciate if you would be good enough to invite Mr. Gross to see you at your convenience with a view to helping him obtain suitable employment."

BLIND EDUCATION

Living in Moscow under Communism, Refoel Kahan helped establish a clandestine network of religious schools. At the end of 1930, he met the same fate as many who defied the Soviet government; the father of four was separated from his family and sent to a labor camp in Siberia.

It was then that his wife, Rivkah Kahan, began to lose her eyesight. The family begged her to consult an eye doctor, but she refused. She was afraid a doctor would deem her unfit to care for her family and report her to the Soviet authorities, who would place her children in state-led orphanages.

Her dedication to her children cost her dearly. In 1935, when her husband was freed and the family immigrated to Israel (then Palestine), she was practically blind.

"Although she couldn't see," said her granddaughter Tziri Livnoni, "she was still fully aware of the family's needs. She always had the most comforting words for someone in distress or needing advice."

She remembered how her grandmother would sit quietly in the corner of the kitchen, listening carefully to the conversation around her before offering her own perspective. "Above all, she knew how to deliver a deep concept in Chassidic philosophy to us. She would explain every detail in such clarity."

In Israel, the family endured much poverty. Once, their daughter Gita arrived home from school and announced that her class was going on a field trip for which each student was required to pay a small fee. But even such a minor expense was beyond the family's ability.

To allay her disappointment, her parents offered an exchange. "We cannot give you money," they told her, "but if it will make you happy, we will host a Chassidic gathering for your friends this Shabbos." The young Gita eagerly accepted. She loved the singing, the stories, and the atmosphere at the gatherings.

"This immediately calmed me down," she would tell her children many years later.

THE CHIEF
RABBI'S COUSIN

He had a fiery character, a sharp tongue, and an eye that saw through every kind of deception. Rabbi Mordechai Eliyahu (1929–2010) was the chief rabbi of Israel, and as such, sat on the board that selected rabbinical judges and pulpit rabbis.

As is often the case, these positions were easier to obtain when there was someone to advocate for you on the board. But young rabbis who had toiled in their studies knew that they would find an impartial judge in the chief rabbi, who was known for evaluating each person based on their personal merits.

Indeed, the chief rabbi's family members knew not to expect any extra help.

So when Rabbi Eliyahu stood up during a meeting and announced that he had a relative whom he wished to see appointed to the rabbinical court, everyone was shocked.

The board immediately granted his request, but later, when another member met the newly appointed judge, he could not resist congratulating him on his powerful relative. "Thanks to your relative Rabbi Eliyahu, you received the position."

"There must be some mistake," the man replied. "We are not related."

The news spread quickly, and finally someone summoned the courage to ask the chief rabbi why he had claimed an alliance that didn't exist. Smiling, he said, "I went through the list of candidates. I saw this man's name. I saw that he received good marks, and I knew that he has a large family to feed."

He also knew that the man had no powerful relations who could influence the board. "So I became his relative," he said, and quoted the verse in Proverbs (7:4): "Say to wisdom, 'You are my sister,' and to understanding, 'You are my relation.'" Thus, he concluded, "He is truly my relative."

THE WATER CARRIER'S ARGUMENT

Rabbi Israel Baal Shem Tov, founder of the Chassidic movement, once instructed a disciple who was leaving town to stop at the home of a water carrier named Michel in Zolochiv, Ukraine, and give him his regards.

The disciple was pleased and proud. After all, the water carrier must be an exceptional person to merit such an honor.

Accordingly, he sought Michel out and delivered Rabbi Israel's message. The poor man received it with joy, and in honor of the occasion, prepared a festive lunch for the guest consisting of two small fish.

Michel's children had hidden themselves when the guest entered so that he would not see their impoverished state. In a whisper, they told each other that the stranger certainly would not finish his portion, so they would have some leftovers to eat as well.

Overhearing them, Rabbi Israel's disciple was so distressed that he began to cry.

"Why are you crying?" the water carrier asked.

"The poverty here is painful to see."

Michel then told him the following story: A rich family was marrying off their daughter and invited all of the town's poor to the wedding feast. But during the ceremony, the bride fainted under the canopy and died suddenly. Havoc ensued, and a debate commenced amongst the poor people in attendance. Some said they should eat the food, lest it go to waste. Others refused, saying, "Who could eat after such a tragedy?"

The water carrier concluded, "We were in middle of the 'wedding' between the Jewish nation and G-d when the Temple in Jerusalem was destroyed. It's true that I am poor, but what pleasure could riches give me when all my joy has turned to sorrow?"

Providence

PASTRIES AND LOST TEFILLIN

Every time Chabad of Vancouver Island needed refreshments for an event, they had to order from the nearest kosher bakery, in Richmond, some three hours away. Just before a large event where British Columbia Premier John Horgan was expected, they were left in the lurch when the person who had promised to pick up the pastries canceled his trip.

The directors of the Chabad House, Rabbi Meir and Chani Kaplan, were stuck. With no alternative, the rabbi took the last ferry to Richmond. He planned to pick up the pastries first thing in the morning and take an early ferry back home.

At six in the morning, he made his way to the bakery, loaded his car with boxes of pastries, and rushed to catch the nine o'clock ferry. After a quick coffee at the terminal, he prepared for morning prayers and looked for the small suitcase where he kept his tefillin. But the bag was gone.

He suddenly recalled that when he was loading the car, he had removed his suitcase to make room for the boxes and forgotten it on the sidewalk outside the bakery. Several frantic phone calls later, it was still missing.

Rabbi Kaplan returned home, used his son's tefillin, and forced himself to continue with preparations for the event. But that night, after the event, he tossed and turned, berating himself for his negligence.

The next morning, he received a call from a number he didn't recognize. "Is this Meir Kaplan? My name is Juan. I found your suitcase next to a bakery in Richmond . . ."

The rabbi was overjoyed.

He asked Juan to send the suitcase by courier, and he would cover the costs.

"I'm actually on a tour of British Columbia," Juan said, "and plan to visit the Island on Sunday. I'd be happy to meet you and personally return your suitcase."

On Sunday morning, a Mexican tourist arrived at the Chabad House. The rabbi thanked him profusely, explaining that the suitcase contained sacred objects used during daily prayers.

"I know what tefillin are," Juan said, "and I know how important they are to you. In fact, my great-grandmother was Jewish."

He explained that his great-grandmother had immigrated to Mexico and married a Catholic man. Since then, the family had been practicing Catholics, but he had always maintained an interest in her heritage.

Rabbi Kaplan, aghast, told Juan that he is, in fact, Jewish. "What unbelievable divine providence brought us together!" the rabbi exclaimed. "Would you like to put on tefillin?"

"I would be honored," Juan replied.

IN THE CHINESE WILDERNESS

With no worries, obligations, or time restraints, Ido was hitchhiking across China. Each morning, he awoke in a different hostel and decided where he was going next. "It was my type of fun," he recalled.

One day, he decided to travel to Chengdu, a city some 120 miles away. Much of the route was via dirt roads and dangerous terrain, but Ido was up for a challenge. After trekking for a while, he hitched a ride.

The trip proved too difficult for the truck, however, and the driver told Ido he would have to turn back. Undaunted, twenty-two-year-old Ido continued on foot. Some twenty minutes later, he found himself alone in a large field. He must have taken a wrong turn, but he had no idea where to retrace his steps, or even if he could.

He put down his backpack and took out some water. At that moment, he recalled that when he was a young boy in Jerusalem, a rabbi from the north of Israel had visited his class and taught the children a song, which translated roughly as, "What was, was. The objective now is to begin from the beginning." The long-forgotten song seemed to encapsulate his current situation, and alone in the field, Ido began to sing and dance. "*Mah shehaya, hayah. . . .*"

Just then, a truck rolled up. The driver, surprised to see a young man dancing on his own in a vast field, asked him what he was doing. Ido explained that he was making his way to Chengdu on foot and had lost his way.

"Why are you dancing?" the driver asked.

This is a Jew's way of asking G-d for help, the Israeli explained. Bemused, the driver offered to take him the rest of the way.

The man, a Chengdu resident, dropped Ido off at the only Jewish building he knew of in the city, the Chabad House.

Ido, who had no idea what day it was, walked in and found himself in the middle of a Shabbos meal. Standing at the head of the table and addressing the crowd was the rabbi's grandfather Rabbi Yitzchok Grossman, chief rabbi of the northern Israeli city of Migdal HaEmek.

Ido was shocked to see that it was the same rabbi who had visited his classroom so many years before and taught him the song he had been singing in the field.

"I saw G-d's hand at work in China," he said.

A few weeks later, Rabbi Dovi Henig, Chabad representative in Chengdu, received a text message from Ido: "Can you tell me what time Shabbat begins this week?"

G-D'S DEBT
TO A SICK MAN

As a new Chabad emissary to Toronto in the year 2000, Rabbi Nechemia Deitsch rotated among the three synagogues within walking distance of his home each Shabbos. One week, he made the twenty-minute walk to Shaarei Tzedec, where he found the congregation just sitting down to the third meal of the day. When he declined their invitation to ritually wash his hands for bread, citing the Chabad custom not to do so, a debate erupted, with some arguing that Chabad should not forego such an important mitzvah.

Sholom Langner, a longtime resident of the city, stood up and said, "Let me tell you a story."

In February of 1950, the front page of Toronto's Yiddish newspaper announced the passing of the sixth Lubavitcher Rebbe, Rabbi Yosef Yitzchok. The headline caught his eye, Sholom recalled, because he had heard about Rabbi Yosef Yitzchok from his father, Rabbi Solomon Langner.

Sholom purchased the paper and brought it to his father, who sighed, "Mr. Silver from down the block will sadly pass away this year."

When Sholom asked what the connection was, his father told him that in the summer of 1942, Chaim Silver had become gravely ill. His distraught family, hoping for a miracle, had turned to Rabbi Moshe Langner for a blessing.

The rabbi declined to give a blessing, however. He reminded them that Chaim's father had been a Lubavitcher disciple and encouraged the family to write to Rabbi Yosef Yitzchok, who had recently arrived in New York.

The family called Rabbi Yosef Yitzchok's office and received this response: "Since one angel [of death] is not comparable to 1,000, the family should do something with the number 1,000." Rabbi Yosef

Yitzchok suggested they give 1,000 dollars to the Lubavitch yeshiva that had just opened in Montreal, "and this will stand in good stead for Mr. Silver."

The Silvers immediately committed to donate the money; however, they debated as to when it should be given. Mrs. Silver wanted to give it immediately, but Mr. Silver's brother and business partner balked. "Are you crazy? This is a huge sum of money. There will be plenty of time to make the donation if and when my brother recovers," he argued.

Indeed, Chaim's medical situation improved. That autumn, Chaim received a letter from Rabbi Yosef Yitzchok. "Thank G-d your heart is strengthened and your health improved. You should strengthen your belief and trust in G-d, and G-d should send you a recovery . . . and you should follow the doctors' advice and rest." Then Rabbi Yosef Yitzchok turned to the family's pledge to the yeshiva, relating a story about his father, Rabbi Sholom Dovber:

> *A Jew who was very ill once wrote to my father, promising that if he recovered, he would give*

*a large donation to the yeshiva in the town of
Lubavitch. My father sent his blessing for a full
recovery and wrote to him, "In regard to your
commitment to the yeshiva, it is better that you
should fulfill the pledge immediately, and G-d
will be your debtor, rather than you being a
debtor to G-d."*

Rabbi Yosef Yitzchok concluded by remind-
ing Chaim not to take G-d's blessings for granted.
"When a person contemplates how, though he is
lowly, he can still give G-d spiritual pleasure . . . he
must be immensely joyous. And this holy joy is a
pure vessel for health and good livelihood."

The letter convinced Mrs. Silver that the donation should be made immediately, and she sent her
son to Montreal with a check. Chaim fully recovered from his illness and lived several more years,
but as Rabbi Langner had predicted, he died shortly
after Rabbi Yosef Yitzchok in 1950.

The crowd at Shaarei Tzedec listened atten-
tively. The discussion surrounding Chabad practice
resolved peacefully, and they parted warmly after
Shabbos.

The very next day, Rabbi Deitsch was reading a volume of Rabbi Menachem Mendel's published letters and found a letter written to Sholom's father. Over a decade after the passing of Rabbi Yosef Yitzchok, Rabbi Langner had written the story of Mr. Silver's recovery and passing to Rabbi Menachem Mendel.

Rabbi Menachem Mendel took issue with Rabbi Langner's assumption that Mr. Silver's blessing had expired when Rabbi Yosef Yitzchok passed away. "The blessings of the righteous are everlasting and have their desired effect," he wrote, "and especially according to what our sages say (*Zohar* 280a), that the righteous who pass away are even more accessible to the living than during their lifetimes . . . ."

ONE MORE GIFT

When the Brazilian television station Confederação Israelita do Brasil asked the Weitmans if they would agree to appear on a show about Jewish life, the couple hesitated. They worried that a journalist might misconstrue their words. But, upon hearing that they were the only observant family to be featured, they agreed. After all, presenting this particular approach to Jewish life was part of their work as Chabad representatives in the country.

On the scheduled day, a camera crew arrived in the neighborhood and asked a child if he knew where the Weitman home was located. Yes, he replied, it was his house, and just two blocks away.

Moments later, they asked a young girl for directions. She replied that she, too, was a Weitman, and directed them to the house. When they arrived, there were several more children playing outside.

With the cameras rolling, the reporter asked the couple how many children they had. Nine, came the reply.

"Why raise such a large family?" the journalist pressed.

"Every child is a present from G-d," they said. "We are joyous at every gift G-d gives us."

Close to a decade later, at a community event, a woman approached Rabbi Weitman. Pointing to a little girl next to her, she said, "This is my daughter. It is because of you that she is alive."

The rabbi, having just met this woman for the first time, was stunned and curious.

"When I was pregnant with my daughter," she explained, "my husband and I decided that we were not ready for another child. We made an appointment for an abortion and were preparing ourselves emotionally for the procedure. The night before the abortion, we were watching television, and a documentary on Jewish life was screening."

As assimilated Jews, she said, they had been interested to see how the secular media would portray them. Then the Weitman family appeared. Like the camera crew, she and her husband were initially shocked at the size of their family. But the Weitmans' response about each child being a gift struck a chord.

"We looked at each other and decided right then and there that we would accept G-d's gift with joy. We canceled the appointment."

G-D CANNOT
BE BURNED

In the middle of the night, a fire broke out in the village of Kaliska (today in Poland). Many homes burned to the ground, among them the house of the famed Chabad disciple Shmuel Munkes. Thankfully, the family awoke in time to escape the flames.

The next morning, Shmuel, who was known for his sharp wit, went to assess the damage. A group of locals accompanied him, knowing that his reaction would be worth observing.

A few charred objects, barely distinguishable amid the ashes, were all that remained of the family's worldly belongings. Shmuel looked at the devastation before him and began to recite a blessing aloud, with great fervor, "Blessed are You . . . King of the Universe. . . ."

The observers expected him to conclude with, "Blessed is the True Judge," a blessing reserved for painful occasions, but they were wrong.

"For not making me a gentile!" Shmuel concluded, to the puzzlement of all.

He looked up and explained, "Could you imagine if I were a gentile, and my idols were burned with my home? That would indeed be a catastrophe. But since I am a Jew, I am grateful that the Supreme Creator I pray to and serve is eternal and cannot burn with my home. And G-d, who is all-encompassing and eternal, will surely not leave me with nothing."

GLOSSARY

Chabad. An acronym for the Hebrew words *chochmah*, *binah*, and *daas* (wisdom, understanding, and knowledge). Chabad is a branch of the Chassidic movement that takes an intellectual approach to the service of G-d. In the second half of the twentieth century, Chabad became known for its dedication to bolstering Jewish observance. See also Lubavitch.*

Chanukah. The eight-day holiday celebrating the rededication of the Holy Temple in Jerusalem in the second century BCE, observed by kindling an additional light on a nine-branched candelabra (menorah) each night.

Chassidism. From the Hebrew word *chassid* (pious), the Chassidic movement was founded in the eighteenth century by Rabbi Israel ben Eliezer, known as the Baal Shem Tov. Chassidic teachings (*Chassidus*) use the mystical writings of the Kabbalah to illuminate the deeper significance of Jewish prayer and observance. A Chassid serves G-d with love and joy, recognizing the role of divine providence in every aspect of his or her life.

esrog. Citron used during the festival of Sukkos* to perform the mitzvah* of the Four Kinds.

kosher. "Fit" (Hebrew). Refers to food that is prepared according to the Jewish dietary laws.

Lubavitch; Lubavitcher. Literally "the town of love," Lubavitch is the name for the Russian village where the Chabad movement was based for over a century. The movement, its followers, and leaders became known as "Lubavitch" or "Lubavitchers." See also Chabad.*

matzah. Unleavened, cracker-like bread eaten during Passover. It commemorates the Exodus from Egypt, when the Jews fled in such haste that they did not have time to let their bread rise.

mitzvah. A commandment. The Torah* contains 613 mitzvahs. The word is also used loosely for any good deed.

pan. An acronym for *pidyon nefesh*, "redemption of the soul" (Hebrew). A letter, usually containing a request for blessings, given to a rebbe* or torn and placed at his gravesite.

Purim. The joyous holiday commemorating the Jews' salvation from Haman's plot to annihilate them in Persia, in the year 3406/355 BCE.

rebbe. "Teacher" (Hebrew). The term also refers to a Chassidic leader.

rebbetzin. The honorary title for the wife of a rabbi.

Shabbos. The Jewish Sabbath, which commemorates the completion of the Six Days of Creation and G-d's resting on the seventh day. It is observed each week from sunset on Friday until Saturday night with festive meals and special prayer services. Weekday activities such as driving, writing, and cooking are prohibited on Shabbos.

Shema. The daily declaration of faith and the unity of G-d, "Hear, O Israel," recited in the morning and evening prayers and before retiring for the night.

Sukkos. The eight-day festival that follows the High Holy Days of Rosh Hashanah and Yom Kippur, celebrated by dwelling in a sukkah and the mitzvah* of the Four Kinds.

tefillin. Black leather boxes containing parchment scrolls worn by Jewish males, beginning two months before their bar mitzvah, on the arm and the head during weekday morning prayers in fulfillment of the command, "You shall bind them as a sign upon your hand, and they shall be for you a reminder between your eyes" (Deuteronomy 6:8).

Torah. The Bible (Five Books of Moses); the Torah scroll; used loosely for the general corpus of Jewish teachings.

yeshiva. "To sit" (Hebrew). Traditionally, the term referred to a higher academy of Torah* study. Today, any Jewish day school or academy may be called a yeshiva.

ACKNOWLEDGEMENTS

It has been over two years since I began writing a weekly story. I started with the intention of gathering all the scraps of paper, notes on my computer, and creased pages littering my desk, and turning them into coherent narratives. I thank G-d for helping me make this possible.

I heard most of these stories firsthand, from a family member or someone who was present at the time, and in many instances I sought out supporting documentation. I thank all those who took the time to share their stories with me.

I also turned to several published books, including Refoel Kahan's *Shmuos V'Sipurim*, Yoel Kahan's *Bedarkei HaChasidim*, Mottel Shusterman's *L'man Yeidu*, and Yehudah Chitrik's *Reshimas Devorim*.

Many stories were omitted because they could not be verified adequately, or were proven to be untrue. It is my hope that all the stories written here are factual.

For flow and ease of reading, I have chosen to not include titles for people depicted, unless there was an official title (like rabbi or rebbetzin). I hope that this will not be viewed as disrespect, but rather as a literary convention.

I thank Rabbi Aaron Raskin, who has been a sounding board for many of these stories; the many who commented on the stories published weekly, specifically Mica Soffer and the COL staff; the staff of Hasidic Archives, chief among them Yitzchok Cohen, for keeping me on track; Sarah Ogince and Chana Lewis-Silberg for fine-tuning the stories; Mimi Palace for proofreading; and my son Meir for the final review. I'm also grateful to Leah Caras of Carasmatic Design for the classy design, and to all those who contributed funds to make this book possible.

Above all, I thank my wife for her patience, especially when I rushed to make deadlines.

This year, my sweet uncle Moshe Zaklikofsky passed away. He lived a life of challenge, but was thankful for it all. After his first battle with a brain tumor, he would often say, "Today is another gift from G-d." It is an honor to dedicate this book in his memory.

In honor of the bar mitzvah of

הבחור התמים

יעקב מנחם מענדל הכהן שי'

בן מלכה צבי'ה שתחי'

*Make your Torah study a
permanent fixture of your life.
Say little and do much.
And receive every man with
a pleasant countenance.*

Ethics of our Fathers 2:15

In honor of

Shloimy and **Mirele
Greenwald**

Dedicated to

our children and grandchildren שיחיו

Rabbi Zushe and **Esther**

Wilhelm

They should be blessed materially and
spiritually with all of their hearts' desires
and much nachas from their
children and grandchildren.

In honor of our children

Mendel, Motti and **Esther**

By their parents
Itchy and **Shaina**
Glassner

In memory of
our dear friend

Shneur Hirsch

שניאור זלמן ע"ה

בן יבלחט"א

אברהם גימפל שי'

By the **Modway** team

In honor of the bar
mitzvah of

Aryeh

By his parents

Sholom and **Kayla**

Kramer

In honor of the bar mitzvahs of

Motti

ברוך מרדכי

Meir

חיים מאיר

and the bas mitzvah of

Shaina

שיינא חוה

שיחיו

Zaklikowski

Photo: Menachem Serraf

About the Author

Dovid Zaklikowski was born in the Crown Heights neighborhood of Brooklyn, New York. He began his writing career at the age of sixteen while studying at the Rabbinical College of America. Since then, he has written thousands of articles, with a focus on Jewish history.

His articles have appeared in, among others, The Jewish Journal, Mishpacha Magazine, Hamodia, The Jewish Advocate, Ami Magazine and the Jewish Standard.

He is the author of over twenty books, including *Footprints: Colorful Lives, Huge Impact* and *Kaleidoscope: Uplifting Views on Daily Life*.

Dovid lives in Brooklyn with his wife, Chana Raizel, and their five children, Motti, Meir, Shaina, Benny, and Mendel. He can be reached at DovidZak@Gmail.com.